ASQ's Pocket (

I0014859

ARTIFICIAL INTELLIGENCE FUNDAMENTALS

Jayet Moon

QUALITY PRESS

Milwaukee, Wisconsin

American Society for Quality, Quality Press, Milwaukee 53203
© 2025 by Quality Press.
All rights reserved. Published 2025
Printed in the United States of America

29 28 27 26 25 LS 5 4 3 2 1

Publisher's Cataloging-in-Publication data

Names: Moon, Jayet, 1988-, author.
Title: Artificial intelligence fundamentals / Jayet Moon.
Series: ASQ's Pocket Guide Series
Description: Includes bibliographical references. | Milwaukee, WI:
  Quality Press, 2025.
Identifiers: LCCN: 2025934099 | ISBN: 9781636942056 (paperback) |
  9781636942063 (PDF) | 9781636942070 (epub)
Subjects: LCSH Artificial intelligence. | Artificial intelligence—Industrial
  applications. | Production management—Quality control. | BISAC
  TECHNOLOGY & ENGINEERING / Quality Control | COMPUTERS /
  Artificial Intelligence / General | COMPUTERS / Artificial Intelligence /
  Natural Language Processing | COMPUTERS / Data Science / Machine
  Learning | BUSINESS & ECONOMICS / Quality Control | BUSINESS &
  ECONOMICS / Information Management
Classification: LCC Q335.4 .M66 2025 | DDC 006.3—dc23

ASQ advances individual, organizational, and community excellence
worldwide through learning, quality improvement, and knowledge
exchange.

Bookstores, wholesalers, schools, libraries, businesses, and organizations:
Quality Press books are available at quantity discounts for bulk purchases
for business, trade, or educational uses. For more information, please contact
Quality Press at 800-248-1946 or books@asq.org.

To place orders or browse the selection of all Quality Press titles,
visit our website at: http://www.asq.org/quality-press.

Quality Press
600 N. Plankinton Ave.
Milwaukee, WI 53203-2914
Email: books@asq.org
Excellence Through Quality™

Contents

List of Figures and Tables

Acknowledgments

I'd like to foremost thank Lillian McAnally for her backing and encouragement for a timely book on such a critical topic. Additionally, this book would not have been possible without selfless support on the home front from Sunil, Shruti and Sweta Desai. Finally I'd like to thank Erica Barse for her editorial assistance and Arun Mathew for his subject matter expertise.

CONTRIBUTORS' ACKNOWLEDGMENTS

The American Society for Quality and Quality Press would like to thank the Quality Press Peer Review Committee for its invaluable volunteer participation and contributions to this work. Without our volunteers' subject matter expertise, time, and passion for creating content, none of our efforts would be possible.

Quality Press Peer Review Committee Members

Scott A. Laman, Chair

Peter Pylipow, Vice Chair

Melvin Alexander

Lance Coleman

Ahmad Elshennawy

Marc Hamilton

Gary Jing

Trevor Jordan

Jane Keathley

Mary McShane-Vaughn

Jayet Moon

G.S. Sureshchandar

Tiea Theurer

Acronyms

AI—Artificial Intelligence

API—Application Programming Interface

AWS—Amazon Web Services

CAPA—Corrective and Preventive Action

CCPA—California Consumer Privacy Act

CNN—Convolutional Neural Network

CT—Cycle Time

DOE—Design of Experiments

ERP—Enterprise Resource Planning

FMEA—Failure Mode and Effects Analysis

GDPR—General Data Protection Regulation

GPT—Generative Pre-trained Transformer

HA—Hazard Analysis

HIPAA—Health Insurance Portability and Accountability Act

HITL—Human in the Loop

IoT—Internet of Things

KPI—Key Performance Indicator

LLM—Large Language Model

LT—Lead Time

MES—Manufacturing Execution System

ML—Machine Learning

NLP—Natural Language Processing

NVA—Non-Value Added

OpenCV—Open Computer Vision Library

OSHA—Occupation Safety and Health Administration

QA—Quality Assurance

QC—Quality Control

PCA—Principal Component Analysis

PDCA—Plan, Do Check, Act

PII—Personally Identifiable Information

PLC—Programmable Logic Controller

RCA—Root Cause Analysis

RFE—Recursive Feature Elimination

RPN—Risk Priority Number

RUL—Remaining Useful Life

SHAP—SHapley Additive exPlanations

SCAR—Supplier Corrective Action Request

SOP—Standard Operating Procedure

SPC—Statistical Process Control

TAT—Turnaround Time

TIMWOODS (8 Wastes)—Transportation, Inventory, Motion, Waiting, Overproduction, Overprocessing, Defects, Skills underutilization

TPS—Toyota Production System

TQM—Total Quality Management

VA—Value Added

VR—Virtual Reality

VSM—Value Stream Mapping

Introduction

"The future belongs to those who understand artificial intelligence and its implications."

– Sundar Pichai

Cars can drive themselves, chatbots can write poems, computer programs can interpret your X-ray or CT scan, similar programs can create new drug candidates, software can execute millions of stock trades at lightning speed, and adaptive algorithms on our phones continually show us personalized content and advertisements for greatest commercial impact. AI doesn't wear a metallic exoskeleton or wield weapons; instead, it exists in lines of code, neural networks, and algorithms that learn, adapt, and evolve.

This isn't a futuristic dream; it's the quiet revolution happening right under our noses. Artificial intelligence (AI) and machine learning (ML) are not coming—they're already here, threading themselves into the fabric of our daily lives, altering everything we know about how we live, work, and think.

About a decade ago, Dr. Greg Watson coined the term *Quality 4.0* to describe the digital transformation in quality systems. Today it is unquestionable that AI and ML are the crown jewels of that transformation.

This book is your invitation to step into the pulse of this transformation. Whether you're a curious observer, a budding innovator, or a skeptic wary of a world ruled by algorithms, this journey will challenge you to see AI and ML as positive catalysts in your work life, regardless of how small or big the task is.

AI and ML have democratized the 4.0 transformation. Anyone with an internet connection today has access to AI and can start transforming the most minor of tasks. You don't need to solve the biggest problems. In this book, you will see how easily you can become a part of the 4.0 transformation, regardless of your role. You will see that AI and ML touch every aspect of quality and have the potential to improve almost every task in quality management.

Machine learning is not about machines replacing us—it's about machines *amplifying* us, pushing the boundaries of possibility and productivity. In today's world, understanding AI and ML is no longer the province of a select few experts. It has become a new literacy, a fundamental competence for navigating the modern world. Artificial intelligence/machine learning is fast becoming the *sine qua non* of productivity, and soon it will be impossible to talk about quality without AI. Quality professionals need to upskill immediately and equip themselves for this brave new AI-driven world.

With the unceasing hum of data—trillions of signals, images, and numbers flowing across networks—our machines are learning, adapting, and evolving. They are not just tools; they are becoming collaborators, mentors, and even creative partners. As we teach them, they teach us—about complexity, patterns, ethics, and the very nature of intelligence itself.

– Jayet Moon
Newark, Delaware

Chapter 1

Introduction to AI and ML in Quality Management

In the fast-paced and ever-evolving world of quality, maintaining efficiency, accuracy, and innovation is crucial. The rise of artificial intelligence (AI) and machine learning (ML) has ushered in a transformative era for quality professionals and leaders. These advanced technologies are no longer confined to tech industries but have found widespread application across manufacturing, healthcare, software development, and beyond. This chapter introduces the foundational concepts of AI and ML, outlines their relevance to quality management, and sets the stage for their everyday application.

THE NEXT STEP IN THE EVOLUTION OF QUALITY

Quality management has traditionally relied on structured methodologies and frameworks such as plan, do, check, act (PDCA), total quality management (TQM), Juran trilogy, Toyota Production System (TPS), Six Sigma, ISO standards, and Agile and lean principles. These frameworks emphasize consistency, defect prevention, and continuous improvement. All of these approaches unquestionably involve data collection, analysis, and interpretation. These processes can be time-consuming and prone to human error.

AI and ML provide an opportunity to enhance these methodologies and make the work faster, efficient, scalable, and effective. AI algorithms can process large amounts of data at unprecedented speeds, while ML models can learn patterns and predict outcomes helping quality professionals make data-driven decisions. By automating repetitive tasks and providing deeper insights, AI/ML has the potential to amplify the impact of quality management practices. A Quality 4.0 transformation in today's world is impossible without AI/ML.

UNDERSTANDING AI AND ML BASICS

What Is Artificial Intelligence (AI)?

Artificial intelligence refers to the simulation of human intelligence by machines. It is composed of a broad range of capabilities, including problem-solving, decision-making, natural language processing, and vision recognition.

What Is Machine Learning (ML)?

Machine learning, a subset of AI, involves training algorithms to recognize patterns and make predictions based on data that the user feeds to it. ML models improve over time as they ingest more data, making them particularly valuable for identifying trends, anomalies, and opportunities for process improvement.

Key Differences Between AI and ML

While AI refers to the larger concept of an intelligent algorithm that can be within a machine or a system, ML focuses on teaching systems to learn from data. Think of AI as the overall goal of creating intelligent systems and ML as one of the tools to achieve it.

WHY AI/ML MATTERS FOR QUALITY PROFESSIONALS

AI and ML address many of the pain points quality professionals face. These include:

1. Data overload: Modern production and service environments generate massive amounts of data. AI/ML can sift through that data very fast, identifying critical insights quickly and accurately.

2. Error reduction: By automating repetitive and error-prone tasks, AI has the potential to minimize human errors and improve overall accuracy.

3. Predictive insights: ML algorithms analyze historical data to predict future trends, such as potential failures or process inefficiencies, thereby enabling proactive quality management.

4. Increased efficiency: Automation powered by AI can reduce the time spent on manual processes, allowing professionals to focus on strategic initiatives. The human becomes a verifier and double checker instead of the primary creator.

5. Adaptability: As systems evolve, AI/ML models can adapt and remain relevant, providing continuous value without requiring complete overhauls.

6. Turnaround time (TAT): AI/ML can significantly shorten TAT for a variety of tasks, such as data requests, charting, investigation, and analysis.

REAL-WORLD EXAMPLES OF AI/ML IN QUALITY MANAGEMENT

Many organizations today are already harnessing the power of AI/ML. Some real-world examples are listed below.

- Automated visual inspection—manufacturers can use AI-driven computer vision to detect defects in products with higher accuracy and speed than manual inspections.[1]

- Predictive maintenance—ML models can predict equipment failures, allowing for timely maintenance and reducing unplanned downtime.[2]

- Statistical process control (SPC)—AI enhances SPC by connecting with traditional SPC techniques and continuously analyzing production data multidimensionally, identifying trends, and providing real-time alerts for deviations, thereby enabling predictive analytics.[3]

- Customer feedback analysis—sentiment analysis powered by natural language processing (NLP) can help companies identify quality issues from customer feedback and reviews.

Large numbers of customer complaints can be processed with speed, and causes can be determined for targeted mitigations. AI models can help brainstorm root causes, write nonconformances, and even respond to customers.[4]

- Supply chain optimization—AI and ML can enhance supply chain efficiency by predicting disruptions, optimizing inventory management, and improving vendor selection processes. These technologies can help ensure consistent quality by analyzing supplier data and forecasting risks, which significantly reduces lead times and improves TAT.[5]

- Healthcare imaging and drug discovery—AI-driven tools today are already revolutionizing healthcare by enhancing image analysis for diagnostics, such as identifying abnormalities in X-rays or MRIs, with unparalleled speed and accuracy. In drug discovery, ML algorithms can accelerate the identification of potential compounds, simulate molecular interactions, and optimize clinical trial designs, dramatically reducing the time and cost of bringing new drugs to market.[6]

- Data visualization, interpretation, and analysis—AI-powered tools offer intuitive visualizations that transform complex data sets into actionable insights. From real-time dashboards that track key performance indicators (KPIs) to predictive models that identify potential issues, these tools can enable professionals to interpret trends and make data-driven decisions effectively. Additionally, ML algorithms help in uncovering hidden patterns and correlations that might not be immediately apparent through traditional and often manual analysis methods.[7]

- Risk management—By analyzing large volumes of historical and real-time data, AI can identify potential risks on the horizon. ML algorithms assist in performing comprehensive risk assessments, such as hazards analysis (HA) and failure modes and effects analysis (FMEA), by prioritizing risk factors based on their likelihood and impact. AI models can help risk management teams brainstorm causes and controls, including the verification of their effectiveness. Furthermore, AI tools can provide early warnings for quality deviations, enabling proactive mitigation strategies that minimize disruptions and ensure consistent compliance.[8]

As this book unfolds, we will explore how AI and ML can be seamlessly integrated into everyday quality management practices. From process optimization to non-conformance management, and from value stream mapping to reliability engineering, the possibilities are vast. This chapter has detailed the foundation for understanding the transformative potential of these technologies. In the coming chapters, we will dive deeper into specific applications, providing practical guidance and actionable insights for quality professionals.

SELF-DRIVING CARS: HOW TESLA FULL SELF DRIVING (FSD) USES AI

Tesla FSD is a good real-world example of a car powered by AI that utilizes ML, neural networks, and real-time data processing to interpret and navigate complex driving environments. Below are the key AI technologies that enable FSD:

1. Neural networks (NNs)
   - Tesla vehicles with their v12 software update largely rely on custom-designed NNs to process input from their suite of cameras, sensors, and radar (in older models).
   - The NNs analyze this input to:
     - Recognize objects such as vehicles, pedestrians, traffic lights, road signs, and lane markings.
     - Understand spatial relationships and predict the behavior of nearby objects.
2. Vision-based approach
   - Tesla has recently transitioned to a vision-only system called "Tesla Vision," eliminating the use of additional physical radars.

- Eight surround cameras within the car provide a 360-degree view of the environment, capturing high-definition imagery that the AI processes to make real-time driving decisions.

3. Dojo supercomputer

- Tesla developed the Dojo supercomputer, a high-performance computing system to train its AI models.

- Dojo processes massive datasets collected from Tesla vehicles worldwide, enabling faster and more efficient training of neural networks.

4. Real-time data processing

- Tesla vehicles use edge AI to process data locally on the onboard computer, reducing latency and ensuring immediate responses to road conditions.

5. Machine learning and model training

- Tesla uses supervised learning to train its models by labeling real-world driving data.

- The system is constantly improving through fleet learning, where millions of Tesla vehicles collect driving data that are sent back to Tesla's servers for analysis and refinement.

6. Prediction and planning algorithms

- Tesla FSD uses AI to predict the behavior of other road users, such as cars and pedestrians.

- These predictions guide planning algorithms to make safe and efficient driving decisions.

Chapter 2

The Foundations of AI and ML for Quality Professionals

As quality professionals begin their journey with AI and ML, understanding the foundational concepts is crucial. This chapter delves into the core principles of AI and ML, introduces key terminologies, and explores how data serve as the backbone of these technologies. Armed with this knowledge, quality professionals can effectively integrate AI and ML into their quality management practices. Let us first review the history of AI before diving deep into AI/ML types and components therein.

HISTORY

Alan Turing's famous paper, "Computing Machinery and Intelligence" (1950)[1], philosophically addresses the question, "Can machines think?" by exploring the potential for AI. Turing introduces the "Imitation Game" (now known as the Turing test) to replace the vague question of whether machines can think. The test involves a human interrogator attempting to distinguish between a human and a machine based solely on their written responses. If the machine's answers are indistinguishable from the human's, it is said to exhibit intelligence. Turing suggests that instead of programming machines with all possible knowledge, they should be built to learn from experience, much like a child. This early insight into ML emphasizes adaptive systems that improve over time. Turing's paper is a foundational work in AI and computer science. The Turing test remains a widely discussed benchmark for evaluating machine intelligence, even as AI has evolved beyond the frameworks he proposed.

In 1956, John McCarthy, Marvin Minsky, Nathaniel Rochester, and Claude Shannon organized the Dartmouth Summer Research Project on Artificial Intelligence, a pivotal event that marked the formal beginning of AI as a field of study. The conference aimed to explore the idea that machines could simulate human intelligence, focusing on topics such as reasoning, problem-solving, language understanding, and learning. Participants developed foundational concepts like symbolic reasoning and heuristic search, and proposed that human cognition could be modeled using computational methods. This gathering not only coined the term "artificial intelligence," but it also set the research agenda that shaped the future of AI development.

Deep Blue, developed by IBM in the 1990s, marked a pivotal paradigm shift in AI by demonstrating the power of specialized AI systems for solving highly complex problems. Unlike general-purpose AI, Deep Blue was a chess-playing supercomputer designed to calculate and evaluate billions of possible moves, leveraging brute-force computation combined with strategic heuristics. In 1997, it achieved a historic milestone by defeating reigning world chess champion Garry Kasparov in a six-game match, showcasing the ability of AI to rival and surpass human expertise in specific domains. This victory underscored the effectiveness of domain-specific AI systems and set the stage for future advancements in ML and specialized problem-solving technologies.

TYPES OF AI

AI encompasses a wide range of technologies that enable machines to perform tasks traditionally requiring human intelligence. These tasks include problem-solving, decision-making, pattern recognition, natural language processing, and understanding. On a macro level, AI can be classified into the following buckets:

- Artificial narrow AI: Designed to perform a specific task (for example, image recognition, language processing, or language translation), it usually is unable to perform tasks outside of its core commands. For example, OpenAI's ChatGPT, IBM Watson, and Amazon Alexa are narrow AIs. Most AI applications in quality management fall under this category.[2]

- General AI: Hypothetical AI capable of performing any intellectual task a human can do, general AI is capable of using previous learnings to perform new tasks. Neural networks are one possible way to achieve general AI.[3]

- Super AI: An advanced form of AI surpassing human intelligence in all areas, super AI is currently the realm of speculation and science fiction.[4]

Types of Narrow AI

There are two types of AI we are interested in: predictive and generative (Figure 2.1). Predictive AI can make classifications, do pattern detection, and predict outcomes based on input information within the defined domain. Generative AI is capable of generating entirely new outputs rather than relying solely on prior data patterns. This creative power of AI is what's spurring the new AI revolution led by large language models (see Appendix A). Generative AI can unlock thousands of hours of productivity from knowledge workers by freeing them from routine computational tasks. It can generate code, write magazine articles, create tutorials, and even deliver commentary on items such as X-ray images, manufacturing defects, and research papers.

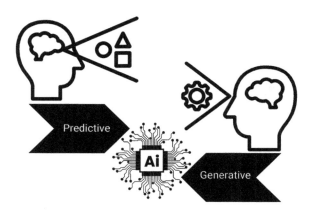

Figure 2.1   Types of narrow AI.

What is Machine Learning?

Machine learning (ML) is a subset of AI that enables systems to learn from user-fed data rather than being explicitly programmed. ML models identify patterns and make predictions or decisions based on input data, and their accuracy improves as they are exposed to more data.

TYPES OF MACHINE LEARNING

There are three main categories of ML:

1. Supervised learning

   - The model learns from user-labeled data, where input-output relationships are clearly defined such that the model can then label or categorize new data points as taught.

   - It is often used for classification or regression tasks such as using ChatGPT for analyzing complaint data.[5]

2. Unsupervised learning

   - The model groups unlabeled data (without human labeling help) based on similarity to identify patterns or groupings.

   - It is often used for clustering and dimensionality reduction tasks such as identifying anomalies in production data or clustering customer feedback.[6]

3. Reinforcement learning

   - The model learns through trial and error by receiving rewards or penalties for actions.

   - It is often used for optimizing complex manufacturing processes or robotic process automation.[7]

Sometimes, a fourth type of ML is identified as semi-supervised learning. As the word suggests, this is a combination of supervised and unsupervised learning. This has great use cases where there is partial availability of labeled data. The remaining unlabeled data can be used to predict patterns within expected variables or are labeled by the model by learning on the partially labeled data.

NATURAL LANGUAGE PROCESSING AND LARGE LANGUAGE MODELS

Large language models (LLMs) are a type of advanced AI that form the backbone of tools like ChatGPT. These models are designed to process and generate human language using billions (or even trillions) of parameters, enabling them to understand context, generate coherent text, and perform complex tasks like summarization, translation, and conversational interaction.

Natural language processing (NLP) is a branch of AI that focuses on enabling LLMs to understand, interpret, and generate human language. It is a combination of supervised learning (for tasks like classification, sentiment analysis, and language translation) and unsupervised learning (for clustering, topic modeling, and semantic analysis). Advanced NLP models, like ChatGPT, utilize generative AI to create new outputs based on learned patterns, making them capable of handling conversational and context-rich tasks effectively.

Generative AI models powered by NLP are particularly adept at leveraging contextual embeddings and transformer-based architectures. This allows them to go beyond basic rule-based language understanding and instead create meaningful, human-like interactions. For instance, ChatGPT uses a pre-trained transformer model to understand nuanced queries, interpret user intent, and produce detailed and relevant responses. This blend of supervised learning, unsupervised learning, and generative capabilities makes NLP a revolutionary tool across industries, particularly in applications such as virtual assistants and automated reporting.

What Sets LLMs Apart?

Large language models are built on transformer architectures, such as OpenAI's GPT series, which allow the models to:

1. Understand context. By analyzing input text as sequences, LLMs grasp the relationships between words and phrases, considering the broader context of a conversation or document.

2. Generate natural language. These models are generative AI systems, capable of producing entirely new text that aligns with input prompts and learned patterns.

3. Scale through pretraining and fine-tuning. LLMs undergo pretraining on vast amounts of text data to learn general language structures, followed by fine-tuning on specific datasets for domain expertise. You will see how to do this yourself later in the book!

Large Language Models in Action

For example, an LLM like GPT-4 can:

- Answer questions—provide detailed, context-aware answers to user queries.

- Generate content—create blog posts, images, charts, diagrams, emails, or even technical documentation.

- Analyze language—perform sentiment analysis, topic classification, or keyword extraction.

Role of LLMs in Customizing ChatGPT

When customizing ChatGPT, LLMs enable tailoring through methods like:

1. Prompt engineering, such as modifying inputs to guide responses (for example, instructing ChatGPT to adopt a specific tone or persona). See Chapter 5.

2. Fine-tuning, or training and modifying the pre-trained model on proprietary datasets to specialize in a domain, specific data set, or task, such as legal, medical, or technical support.

3. Adding knowledge sources, such as augmenting the pre-trained AI model with external databases or domain-specific knowledge for enhanced relevance.

Strengths of LLMs

The benefits of using LLMs include:

- Scalability—they handle vast datasets and complex queries with ease.
- Adaptability—they can be applied to a variety of domains with appropriate fine-tuning.
- Generative power—they produce unique and contextually accurate text outputs.

Challenges

Despite their power, LLMs face challenges such as:

- Bias in outputs—if training data contain biases, the model may replicate them.
- Data privacy—using sensitive information in LLMs requires compliance with internal and external company data protection standards.
- Computational requirements—training and deploying LLMs demands significant hardware and energy resources, and thereby that may incur costs.

BASIC COMPONENTS OF AI/ML SYSTEMS

Figure 2.2 shows the main components that comprise AI/ML systems. These include:

- Data
  - Data provide the foundation of AI/ML. High-quality, relevant data are essential for effective models. The user can feed the model with data of their choice.
- Algorithms
  - These are the mathematical instructions that define how the model learns and makes predictions. Lay users usually

will need help to modify algorithms; therefore, be careful when choosing your model.

- Training and testing
  - Training data are used to teach the model. The user should carefully vet the data before uploading.
  - Testing data or selected data are used to evaluate the model's performance on unseen data. Users should have inputs and outputs defined.
- Model evaluation
  - Determine how well a model performs. The user should analyze model outputs and tweak parameters until the expected acceptable range of outputs is available. Examine metrics such as accuracy, precision, recall, and F1-score.

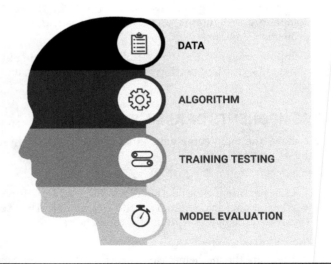

Figure 2.2   Key components of AI/ML systems.

THE MODEL

A model in the context of AI and ML is a mathematical representation of a real-world process or system. It is the result of training an algorithm on data to identify patterns, make predictions, or automate decisions. Models are the functional core of ML applications, translating raw data into actionable insights or automated responses.

How Can We Use a Model?

Models can be used in various ways, depending on their purpose. Some examples include:

- Content generation—generating language content such as articles, codes, failure investigations, diagrams, graphs, summaries of text or data, tutorials, etc.

- Numeric operations—solving algebraic or statistical problems, including coming up with methods and applying them to real-world problems.

- Prediction—forecasting outcomes such as defect rates, equipment failures, or demand trends.

- Classification—categorizing data, such as classifying products as defective or non-defective.

- Optimization—enhancing processes by finding the best combination of variables, such as production speed and resource allocation.

- Anomaly detection—identifying outliers in data, such as detecting quality issues in manufacturing.

Where Do We Get Models?

Models can be obtained in several ways.

- Prebuilt models—many AI platforms (for example, TensorFlow, PyTorch, Azure AI, or AWS SageMaker) provide pre-trained models for common tasks.

- Custom models—these are developed in-house by training algorithms on proprietary data, tailored to specific needs.

- Open-source models—access freely available models from repositories like GitHub or AI model zoos. Additionally, tools like ChatGPT, Copilot, and Gemini offer advanced pre-trained AI models that can be integrated into workflows for tasks such as NLP, predictive analytics, or anomaly detection. These platforms often provide application programming interfaces (APIs) and documentation, making it easier for professionals to implement them in their quality management systems.

How to Set Up a Model

Setting up a model involves several steps:

1. Define objectives. Clearly state the problem the model should solve.

2. Collect data. Gather relevant, high-quality data for training and testing.

3. Select an algorithm. Choose an appropriate algorithm based on the problem type (for example, regression, classification, or clustering).

4. Train the model. Use training data to teach the model how to make decisions or predictions.

5. Validate the model. Evaluate the model's performance using testing data to ensure accuracy.

6. Deploy the model. Integrate the model into your systems or workflows.

7. Monitor performance. Continuously track the model's output and retrain it as needed to maintain effectiveness.

EXAMPLE

An example of a real-life use case of using ChatGPT of Open AI[8] is shown below.

Objective: Improve customer satisfaction by quickly identifying recurring issues, their proper categorization, and their causes from incoming complaint data. This will eliminate hours of manual categorization time, and employees can focus on fixing things rather than data entry.

Workflow:

1. Objectives defined
   - The goal is to categorize customer complaints and identify the most frequent issues.
2. Data preparation
   - Collect complaint data from sources such as customer feedback forms, product performance reports, warranty claims, emails, and call center logs.
   - Pre-process the data by cleaning up inconsistencies (for example, correcting typos and standardizing formats) and converting text into a structured format as far as possible.
3. Model selection
   - Use ChatGPT, a pre-trained NLP model, for text analysis and categorization.
4. Model training
   - Fine-tune ChatGPT with domain-specific data, such as past complaint resolutions, to improve accuracy.
5. Evaluation and validation
   - Test the model by providing a subset of unseen complaints to ensure accurate categorization and insightful analysis.

6. Deployment

- Deploy ChatGPT via an API to analyze incoming complaints in real time and provide categorized summaries.

7. Monitoring and improvement

- Continuously evaluate the system by comparing its outputs to manually categorized complaints, and refine it as needed.

Outcome: ChatGPT identifies recurring issues, such as delayed shipping or product defects, enabling quality teams to prioritize and resolve these problems effectively. It also assists in predicting defect rates and classifying product quality.

THE ROLE OF DATA IN AI AND ML

Data are the lifeblood of AI and ML. In QA/QC applications, data often come from production logs, sensor readings, customer feedback, or quality inspections. Ensuring data quality and consistency is critical for AI/ML systems to deliver reliable results.

Best practices for data management include:

- Data collection
  - Collect data from reliable and diverse sources.
  - Ensure data align with the goals of the quality initiative.
- Data cleaning
  - Remove duplicate, incomplete, or irrelevant entries.
  - Standardize data formats for consistency.
- Data labeling
  - Provide clear labels for supervised learning tasks.
- Data security and compliance
  - Ensure compliance with data privacy regulations such as GDPR or HIPAA.

Conclusion: Building a Strong Foundation

Understanding the foundational concepts of AI and ML is the first step toward leveraging their full potential in quality management. By focusing on data quality, selecting the right models, and addressing common challenges, quality professionals can lay the groundwork for successful AI/ML integration. In the next chapter, we will explore specific AI/ML tools and techniques that can be applied to real-world quality assurance and control tasks.

Chapter 3
Tools and Use Cases for AI/ML in Quality

This chapter explores the practical application of the fundamentals discussed in the previous chapters. Quality professionals must understand the AI/ML methods, tools, and techniques to make the right choice for the quality process at hand. One tool may not fit all quality processes. We will walk through the popular AI models and talk about key features and use cases. As you will see, it is possible to be part of the AI revolution without knowing a single line of code!

POPULAR TOOLS

Figure 3.1 lists the most common AI tools based on coding complexity. These include:

1. ChatGPT and NLP-based tools (see Appendix A for a list)

   - Use case: Extract actionable insights from unstructured data like emails, customer responses, production logs, audit observations, or survey responses.

   - Key features
     - Text summarization and sentiment analysis
     - Automated generation of reports or responses
     - Seamless integration via APIs for real-time processing

   - *Fun fact: ChatGPT reached one million users in five days!*

2. TensorFlow, Keras, and PyTorch

   - Use case: Build and train custom AI/ML models for defect detection, predictive maintenance, or optimization tasks. These are capable of deep learning.

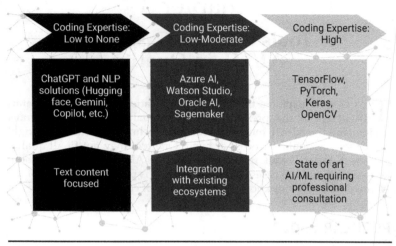

Figure 3.1 Popular AI/ML tools.

- Key features
  - Comprehensive frameworks for supervised, unsupervised, and reinforcement learning
  - Scalability for large datasets
  - Prebuilt models for quick implementation
- *Fun fact: Tesla uses PyTorch for self-driving capabilities.*

3. Azure AI, Watson, Oracle AI, and AWS SageMaker

- Use case: Leverage pre-trained models or deploy custom AI solutions for well-known ecosystems (Microsoft, IBM, Oracle, and Amazon) and IoTs (Internet of Things).
- Key features
  - Cloud-based environments for efficient model training and deployment
  - Integration with IoT devices for real-time quality monitoring

- Power business intelligence (BI) integrations for visualization
- *Fun fact: Sagemaker is named after the sage plant, reflecting its role in cultivating a wise 'sage' AI.*

4. OpenCV

- Use case: Use computer vision for automated visual inspections in manufacturing.
- Key features
  - Image and video analysis for defect detection
  - Object recognition and tracking capabilities
- *Fun fact: The first-ever self-driving car to traverse 100 miles in Mojave in 2005 used OpenCV libraries.*

APPLYING AI/ML IN QUALITY MANAGEMENT

The tools in Figure 3.2 can be used for specific use cases, as detailed below:

1. Predictive analytics

- Purpose: To forecast quality issues before they occur based on past and present data.
- How it works:
  - The AI models are trained on historical production data to predict outcomes like defect rates or equipment failures.
  - An AI model uses real-time data from IoT sensors on the production line to refine predictions.

2. Anomaly detection

- Purpose: To identify deviations from standard processes and labeled outcomes.
- How it works:
  - AI in the form of unsupervised learning algorithms uses "if-then" associations to flag nonstandard inputs coming from production data.
  - An AI model flags anomalies for further investigation to prevent defect propagation.

Figure 3.2 Quality use cases for AI/ML.

3. Natural language processing (NLP)

- Purpose: To analyze unstructured text data like customer reviews or incident reports and provide requested insights.

- How it works:

    - AI models use NLP to extract keywords, classify sentiments, and generate summaries.

    - It is great for using in non-conformances, complaints, corrective and preventive action (CAPA), or supplier corrective action requests (SCARs). Integrate insights into quality improvement plans.

4. Computer vision
   - Purpose: To automate visual inspections and ensure fast and accurate product acceptance.
   - How it works:
     - Train the AI model to recognize defects in real time using labeled images and libraries.
5. Reinforcement learning
   - Purpose: To optimize complex processes such as supply chain logistics or manufacturing schedules.
   - How it works:
     - Train an AI model using trial-and-error methods to maximize efficiency or minimize waste.
     - Provide continual feedback to the AI until optimization is achieved.

CASE STUDY: COMPUTER VISION FOR VISUAL INSPECTIONS

Scenario: A manufacturing company aims to improve its visual inspection process by using AI to detect surface defects on products more efficiently.

Steps to take:

1. Defining objectives
   - Reduce inspection time by 50% and improve defect detection accuracy over manual inspection.
2. Data preparation
   - Capture images of products from production lines, ensuring a diverse dataset with both defect-free and defective samples.
   - Label the dataset for training purposes.

3. Model selection

   - Use OpenCV and TensorFlow to build a convolutional neural network (CNN) for defect detection. *See Appendix B to understand how this can be coded.*

4. Training and validation

   - Train the CNN on labeled images and validate its accuracy on data.

5. Deployment

   - Integrate the trained model into the production line's camera system for real-time inspection.

6. Monitoring and improvement

   - Monitor the model performance continuously, retraining it periodically with new data to adapt to changing defect patterns.

Outcome: The company achieved a 60% reduction in inspection time and a 95% defect detection accuracy, leading to improved product quality and customer satisfaction.

Use best practices for tool and technique selection:

1. Align tools with goals. Choose tools that address specific quality challenges (for example, NLP for text analysis and computer vision for visual inspections).

2. Start small. Begin with pre-built models or simple use cases to build confidence and demonstrate return on investment (ROI) to the organization and leadership.

3. Ensure data readiness. Invest in data cleaning and pre-processing to maximize model effectiveness.

4. Leverage cloud services.

   - Where possible, use cloud-based platforms for scalability and reduced infrastructure costs.

   - This should be balanced against cybersecurity risks.

5. Collaborate with experts. Work with subject matter experts, data scientists, or AI/ML specialists to ensure successful implementation.

Conclusion: Empower Quality Professionals with Tools and Techniques

Planning for AI should be detailed and include as many stakeholders as possible. The planning phase determines what tools and services will be used in the AI transformation project. Quality professionals should weigh the pros and cons of each item under consideration before committing, as these AI models can be expensive. The next chapter will explore how you can create your own personal GPT and get started on your own AI revolution.

Chapter 4

How to Create Your Own ChatGPT Without Coding

The growing accessibility of AI tools via the internet has enabled individuals and organizations to create customized ChatGPT-like models tailored to their specific needs without the use of any coding expertise whatsoever. This chapter provides a comprehensive guide for creating your own ChatGPT-like agent, exploring methods like OpenAI's "My GPT" customization, deploying a model with Azure AI, and using Microsoft Copilot's Studio.

CUSTOMIZING "MY GPT" ON CHATGPT.COM

OpenAI offers an easy way to customize ChatGPT through its "My GPT" feature on ChatGPT.com. This approach allows users to tailor the chatbot's behavior, tone, and knowledge base without requiring programming expertise.

To create your "My GPT" chatbot:

1. Access the "My GPT" feature.

   - Log into your OpenAI account and navigate to the "My GPTs" section.

   - Select "Create My GPT" to start a new customization (Figure 4.1).

2. Define instructions.

   - Specify the behavior and tone for your GPT (Figure 4.2).

   - Example: "Respond professionally and concisely to all technical queries."

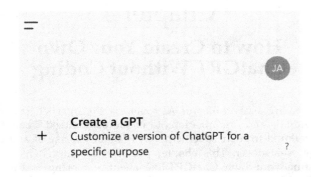

Figure 4.1   Click on "Create a GPT."

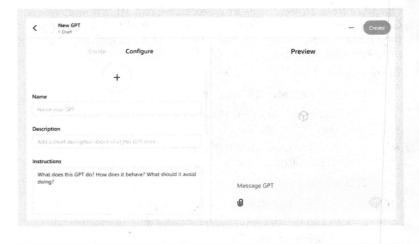

Figure 4.2   Add basic instructions.

3. Add knowledge sources.

- Upload domain-specific documents or provide links for your GPT to reference (Figure 4.3).
- Example: Add company policies and FAQs for an internal support bot.

Figure 4.3　Add knowledge sources.

4. Test and iterate.

- Use the interactive test environment to refine instructions and validate responses.

5. Deploy and share.

- Generate a shareable link to use your GPT or embed it in your workflows.

Advantages of "My GPT":

- Ease of use, which requires no coding or technical expertise
- Focused responses that tailors interactions to specific use cases
- Quick deployment with shareable links to enable immediate use

STEPS TO CREATE YOUR "AGENT" USING COPILOT STUDIO:

1. Access Copilot Studio.

    - Navigate to Copilot Studio and click on "Create."

    - On Create page, select "New Agent" (Figure 4.4).

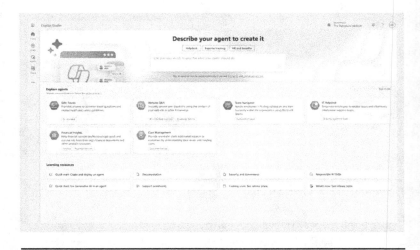

Figure 4.4   Create an agent.

2. Define instructions.

    - Set the behavior and tone of your agent in plain language using chat.

    - Example: Specify, *"Be formal and concise when responding to legal questions."*

3. Add knowledge enhancements.

- In the overview tab in the knowledge section, upload documents or provide links to websites to train your agent on domain-specific information.

- Example: Upload a company's internal standard operating procedures (SOPs) to create an agent trained for customer service queries (Figure 4.5).

Figure 4.5   Add knowledge enhancements.

4. Test and refine.

- Use the testing interface to interact with your agent and fine-tune its behavior by adjusting instructions.

5. Publish your agent.

- At the top of the page, select "Publish," and then select "Publish" again in the "Publish this agent" confirmation message. If the publish is successful, you will see a green banner on the top of the page.

- At the top of the page, select "Go" to demo the website in the overflow menu.

- Send the URL to others to demonstrate it.

USING AZURE AI TO CREATE AND DEPLOY A MODEL

For users who need more control and scalability, Azure AI provides robust tools to create, train, and deploy custom AI models, including GPT-based solutions.

To create and deploy a custom GPT model on Azure:

1. Set up the Azure AI environment.

- Sign in to the Azure Portal.

- Create an Azure AI resource:
  - Search for "Azure OpenAI" in the Azure Marketplace.
  - Click "Create," and configure the resource (for example, region, pricing tier) (Figure 4.6).

2. Access Azure OpenAI Studio or Foundry.

- Navigate to the Azure OpenAI Studio or Foundry Portal and sign in with credentials that have access to your Azure OpenAI resource.

- During or after sign-in, select the appropriate directory, Azure subscription, and Azure OpenAI resource.

3. Use the chat playground.

- From the Azure OpenAI Studio landing page, select "Chat playground" to begin exploring capabilities in a no-code environment (Figure 4.7).

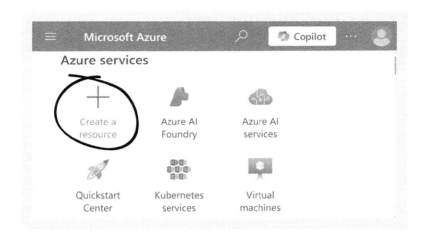

Figure 4.6 Click on "Create a resource."

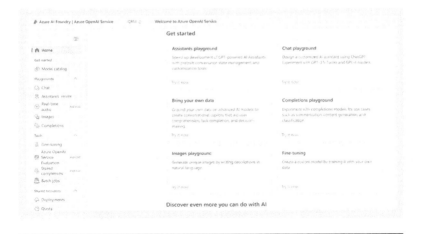

Figure 4.7 Click on "Chat playground."

- Setup: Give the model detailed instructions (Figure 4.8). If you want it to pull from a certain data source, upload the data. For example, define:
  - The assistant's personality
  - What it should or should not answer
  - How responses should be formatted

Figure 4.8   Configure the GPT.

- Key chat playground features
- Adjust key parameters (Figure 4.9) like:
  - Temperature—controls response randomness (higher for creative responses).
  - Max response (tokens)—sets the length of responses.
  - Stop sequences—defines when the model stops responding.

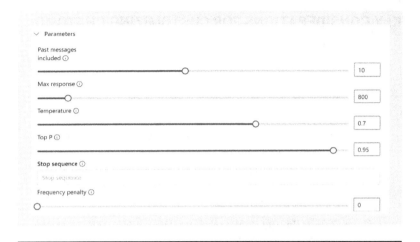

Figure 4.9   Adjust parameters.

- Select "View code" at any point to see Python, curl, or JSON code samples pre-populated for your current chat session and settings.

5. Deploy your model.
   - Once you are satisfied with the experience, select "Deploy to" from the Azure OpenAI Studio.
   - Options for deployment include:
     - Standalone web application—deploy a web app directly with options for new or existing configurations.
     - Copilot in Copilot Studio—deploy as part of an integrated copilot experience if using additional data.
   - Setup. Choose a name for your web app (for example, https://<appname>.azurewebsites.net), subscription, resource group, and pricing tier.

KEY CONSIDERATIONS FOR CUSTOMIZING CHATGPT

1. Data privacy and security

   - Ensure sensitive data are anonymized and stored securely.

   - Use encryption for data are transit and at rest when using APIs.

2. Scalability

   - Use cloud resources (for example, Azure) that can scale with user demand.

   - Implement load balancing and caching for high-traffic applications.

3. Maintenance and updates

   - Regularly update the model with new training data to keep responses accurate.

   - Continually monitor the model's performance and address any inaccuracies or biases by refreshing instructions or knowledge base.

4. Cost management

   - Track usage and optimize resources to minimize operational costs (for example, token tracking and model use).

   - Use features within the model's ecosystem like autoscaling to manage unpredictable traffic patterns.

Conclusion: Building Your Own AI Agent

Creating a custom AI Agent can range from a simple setup using ChatGPT to a more customized model built and deployed with Azure AI. By understanding your objectives, preparing high-quality datasets, and leveraging functionality within the available platforms, you can build an agent tailored to your unique quality needs—whether that's for customer service, internal tools, or industry-specific applications. In the next chapter, we will talk about how to best use this agent (that is, how to talk to it using prompts). This has become a science of its own called *prompt engineering*.

Chapter 5
Mastering Prompt Engineering

Prompt engineering has emerged as a cornerstone skill for interacting with large language models (LLMs). As AI continues to evolve, the ability to craft effective prompts has become essential for extracting accurate, relevant, and creative outputs. This chapter details the principles, techniques, and applications of prompt engineering, equipping you with the tools to communicate effectively with AI systems and LLMs in particular.

UNDERSTANDING THE IMPORTANCE OF PROMPTS

A prompt is the input or instruction given to an AI model to elicit a desired response. The quality of the output is often a direct reflection of the quality of the prompt. LLMs try to anticipate the next word in a sequence based on information provided to them. LLMs try to do what is referred to as "completions," and the better the preceding information, the better the end output of the LLM will be.

To create an effective prompt:

1. Define the context. Provide the model with the necessary background or constraints.

2. Specify tasks. Clearly outline the expected format, tone, or content.

3. Guide creativity. Encourage innovative responses while maintaining relevance.

A well-crafted prompt can make the difference between vague, unhelpful answers and precise, actionable insights.

PRINCIPLES OF EFFECTIVE PROMPT ENGINEERING

To craft high-quality prompts, consider the following principles:

1. Clarity and specificity—be clear and specific about what you want AI to do. Ambiguity will often lead to irrelevant or generic responses.

   - Example: Instead of saying, "Tell me about history of Industrial Revolution," specify, "Provide a summary of the causes and effects of the Industrial Revolution."

2. Provide context—whenever possible, include background information to anchor the response.

   - Example: "As a professional chef, explain the process of making sourdough bread."

3. Use constraints—always limit the scope to ensure relevance and accuracy.

   - Example: "Summarize this text in 100 words or fewer."

4. Iterative refinement—always start with a basic prompt and fine-tune based on the outputs.

   - Example: Adjust "Explain climate change" to "Explain the impact of human activities on climate change in simple terms."

PROMPT TECHNIQUES AND FRAMEWORKS

Consider which prompt may be appropriate for your purposes:

1. Instruction-based prompts. These kinds of prompts explicitly instruct the model on the task.

   - Example: "Write a persuasive essay arguing for renewable energy adoption."

2. Example-based prompts. These kinds of prompts provide examples to guide the model's response style and format.

   • Example: "Translate the following text into French. Example: 'Hello' -> 'Bonjour.' Now translate: 'Good morning.'"

3. Role-play prompts. These kinds of prompts set a role or perspective that helps the AI contextualize the response.

   • Example: "You are a financial advisor. Recommend investment strategies for a beginner."

4. Chain of thought prompts. These kinds of prompts encourage the AI model to reason, step-by-step.

   • Example: "Solve this math problem step-by-step: What is 15% of 200?"

5. Conditional prompts. These kinds of prompts guide responses based on conditions or scenarios.

   • Example: "If the user is a student, explain Newton's laws in simple terms. Otherwise, provide a detailed technical explanation."

COMMON CHALLENGES WITH LLM RESPONSES

An ineffective LLM response may be:

1. Too broad and ambiguous—responses may be too broad or irrelevant.

   • Solution: Fine-tune by narrowing the scope and clarifying intent in the prompt.

2. Lacking in depth—LLM outputs might lack detail or nuance.

   • Solution: Request deeper analysis or specify the desired depth.

3. Short—AI provides very concise answers and does not go beyond a specific length.

   • Solution: Ask for specific word length and also specify the format (bullet points, paragraphs, etc.). If this does not work, break up the requested information into chunks of different prompts and ask AI to collate them at the end.

4. Inconsistent—responses may vary across iterations.

   • Solution: Use precise, detailed, and repeatable phrasing while including examples.

Conclusion

Prompt engineering is both an art and a science, requiring creativity, precision, and adaptability. Iteration and patience are the keys to getting successful outputs from AI. While knowledge base and data that inform AI are important, poor prompt engineering practices will hamper extraction of any meaningful information. Different AI models may need different details based on their underlying instructions. Pretrained models without any user-given instructions need the most detailed prompts, while user-trained agents can often be fine-tuned on the back end to give specific answers for various trigger prompts.

Chapter 6

Integrating AI/ML Solutions into Quality Workflows

AI integration in quality management can be categorized in terms of the complexity of its implementation. We will classify AI integrations into two types in this chapter:

1. Basic—this refers to no code or low code integration that can occur solely with the use of off-the-shelf or lightly modified LLMs using NLP.

2. Advanced—this requires custom-coded solutions, use of IoT, and some capital investment to achieve complex improvements and high-return items, such as predictive analytics and visual inspections.

BASIC AI QUALITY INTEGRATION

Basic application of AI is illustrated in Figure 6.1 and listed below:

1. Acting as a virtual quality assistant

   - ChatGPT,[1] Microsoft Copilot, or similar agents can be deployed as a virtual "chatbot" assistant to handle routine quality queries and tasks.

   - Example: Answering frequently asked questions about quality policies or assisting with calibration scheduling.

2. Enhancing audits and inspections

   - Use ChatGPT or Microsoft Copilot[2] or similar agents to prepare for audits by generating checklists, ensuring audit prep is in alignment with the scope, findings gaps, preparing audit responses, and reviewing previous audit outcomes.

   - Example: Drafting an internal audit checklist based on ISO 9001 standards.

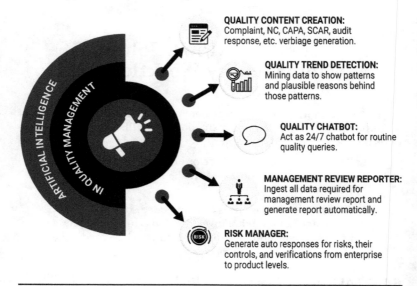

QUALITY CONTENT CREATION:
Complaint, NC, CAPA, SCAR, audit response, etc. verbiage generation.

QUALITY TREND DETECTION:
Mining data to show patterns and plausible reasons behind those patterns.

QUALITY CHATBOT:
Act as 24/7 chatbot for routine quality queries.

MANAGEMENT REVIEW REPORTER:
Ingest all data required for management review report and generate report automatically.

RISK MANAGER:
Generate auto responses for risks, their controls, and verifications from enterprise to product levels.

Figure 6.1 Basic applications of AI in quality.

3. Supporting risk management

- Leverage an agent[3] to brainstorm potential risks and suggest mitigation strategies after feeding it the product or process under analysis.

- Example: Identifying risks in a new production process and proposing controls during a failure mode and effects (FMEA) workshop.

4. Streamlining document reviews

- Automate the review of quality documents for expected items, grammar, clarity, and consistency.

- Example: Reviewing a supplier quality agreement draft and providing suggestions for improvement.

5. Training and knowledge sharing

- Support employee training initiatives and facilitating knowledge sharing.
- Examples:
  - Creating easy-to-understand summaries of complex quality guidelines.
  - Developing quiz questions or training materials for quality management topics.
  - Simulating scenarios for training on handling non-conformances or customer complaints.

6. Improving supplier management

- Enhance supplier quality management and collaboration using NLP-based content analysis.
- Examples:
  - Drafting supplier evaluation forms and contracts.
  - Analyzing supplier performance data and summarizing trends for management review.
  - Automating responses to routine supplier queries about quality requirements.

7. Optimizing non-conformance management

- Simplify handling of non-conformance reports and related tasks.
- Examples:
  - Drafting concise non-conformance descriptions based on input data.
  - Suggesting corrective and preventive actions based on industry best practices.
  - Generating summaries for management review meetings or regulatory reporting.

8. Enhancing continuous improvement

   - Support initiatives aimed at continuous improvement in quality processes.
   - Examples:
     - Providing insights into customer feedback or survey data for process improvements.
     - Proposing ideas for reducing waste or inefficiencies in production workflows.
     - Summarizing trends from internal metrics like defect rates or cycle times.

9. Managing quality metrics and reports

   - Assist in tracking and reporting quality performance metrics.
   - Examples:
     - Automating the generation of monthly or quarterly quality reports.
     - Identifying trends in key performance indicators (KPIs) like defect rates or audit findings.
     - Drafting management review reports with data-driven insights.

10. Enhancing customer complaint handling

    - Streamline the processing and resolution of customer complaints.
    - Examples:
      - Generating automated responses to acknowledge receipt of complaints.
      - Analyzing complaint data to identify recurring issues or patterns.
      - Drafting investigation summaries and proposed resolutions.

11. Assisting change management
    - Facilitate the documentation and implementation of change control.
    - Examples:
        - Drafting change control request forms and impact assessments.
        - Suggesting risk mitigation plans for proposed changes.
        - Reviewing change management documentation for consistency and completeness.

12. Regulatory compliance support
    - Help organizations maintain compliance with quality and regulatory standards.
    - Examples:
        - Summarizing updates to regulations like FDA CFR 21 Part 820 or EU MDR.
        - Creating gap analyses to identify non-compliances in quality systems.
        - Drafting responses to regulatory inquiries or inspection findings.

13. Corrective and preventive actions (CAPA)
    - Streamline CAPA processes by providing templates and automated analyses.
    - Examples:
        - Drafting CAPA plans based on identified root causes.
        - Summarizing CAPA progress and presenting updates for management review.
        - Proposing preventive actions to avoid recurrence of quality issues.

14. Integrating with quality management systems (QMS)

- Integrate ChatGPT-like agents with QMS platforms to enhance efficiency.
- Examples:
  - Providing instant feedback or guidance on navigating QMS modules.
  - Automating data entry for quality records, such as deviations or non-conformance reports (NCRs).
  - Offering proactive alerts for overdue tasks, expiring documents, or pending approvals.

ADVANCED AI QUALITY INTEGRATION

As noted earlier, advanced AI integration in quality management involves custom-coded solutions, IoT-enabled data collection, and significant capital investment to achieve high-value improvements. Unlike basic implementations that largely rely on off-the-shelf LLMs with NLP, advanced integration incorporates ML models for predictive analytics, real-time anomaly detection, inspections using computer vision, and autonomous process optimization and other applications, as shown in Figure 6.2. It enables reduction of defects and compliance enhancement with minimal human intervention. These systems continuously learn from historical and live data, allowing for proactive quality control and self-optimizing workflows that maximize efficiency and return on investment.

Advanced integration models include:

1. Predictive quality analytics

- AI uses historical data and ML models to predict quality issues before they occur.[4]
- Applications:
  - Identifying potential product defects during manufacturing.
  - Forecasting machine failures or process deviations using IoT sensor data.

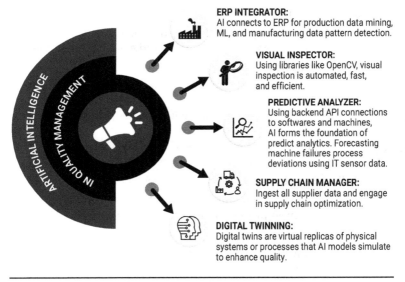

ERP INTEGRATOR:
AI connects to ERP for production data mining, ML, and manufacturing data pattern detection.

VISUAL INSPECTOR:
Using libraries like OpenCV, visual inspection is automated, fast, and efficient.

PREDICTIVE ANALYZER:
Using backend API connections to softwares and machines, AI forms the foundation of predict analytics. Forecasting machine failures process deviations using IT sensor data.

SUPPLY CHAIN MANAGER:
Ingest all supplier data and engage in supply chain optimization.

DIGITAL TWINNING:
Digital twins are virtual replicas of physical systems or processes that AI models simulate to enhance quality.

Figure 6.2 Advanced AI/ML use cases.

- Predicting customer dissatisfaction based on product feedback trends.

2. Computer vision for quality inspections

- AI-powered computer vision systems analyze images or videos to detect defects and ensure product compliance.[5]

- Applications:
  - Automated visual inspections for surface defects, misalignments, or missing components.
  - Real-time monitoring of production lines using AI cameras.
  - Ensuring labeling accuracy, such as checking barcodes or package seals.

3. Autonomous quality audits

- AI automates parts of the internal and external audit process to reduce manual effort and ensure thoroughness.[6]

- Applications:
    - Analyzing audit findings to identify the root causes of non-conformances.
    - Monitoring compliance with regulatory standards in real time using AI tools.
    - Automating checklist generation and sampling plans based on risk levels.

4. Process optimization using reinforcement learning

- AI models continuously learn and optimize manufacturing or business processes based on trial-and-error feedback.[7]

- Applications:
    - Adjusting machine parameters dynamically to maximize product quality.
    - Reducing process variation and enhancing yield in manufacturing.
    - Optimizing workflows in supply chains for consistent quality delivery.

5. Predictive maintenance

- AI predicts equipment failures or degradations to prevent downtime and maintain product quality.[8]

- Applications:
    - Using IoT data to monitor equipment conditions in real time.
    - Implementing maintenance schedules based on usage patterns and predicted wear.
    - Reducing scrap rates by maintaining optimal machine performance.

6. Digital twins for quality monitoring

- Digital twins are virtual replicas of physical systems or processes that AI models simulate to enhance quality.[9]
- Applications:
  - Simulating production processes to identify potential quality issues before implementation.
  - Monitoring and optimizing systems remotely using real-time data feeds.
  - Testing process changes in the virtual twin environment to avoid disruptions.

7. AI-powered supplier quality management

- AI assesses and monitors supplier performance to mitigate risks.[10]
- Applications:
  - Evaluating supplier risk profiles based on historical performance data.
  - Monitoring quality metrics and delivery timelines in real time.
  - Predicting supplier failures or deviations that could impact production quality.

8. Generative design and optimization

- AI generates optimal product designs and manufacturing workflows based on predefined constraints.[11]
- Applications:
  - Reducing material waste while maintaining product strength and quality.
  - Optimizing assembly line layouts for efficiency and error reduction.
  - Enhancing product durability and reliability through simulation-driven design.

9. Autonomous decision support systems

- AI assists decision-making by simulating scenarios and providing actionable recommendations.[12]
- Applications:
  - Evaluating trade-offs between cost, quality, and delivery timelines.
  - Suggesting process improvements based on historical data.
  - Assisting in new product introductions by forecasting potential quality risks.

BENEFITS OF AI FOR QUALITY PROFESSIONALS

Some of the many helpful benefits of AI are:

1. Increased productivity—by automating routine tasks, AIs like ChatGPT allow professionals to focus on strategic initiatives.

2. Improved accuracy—agentic AI minimizes errors in documentation and analysis by offering precise, data-driven insights.

3. On-demand expertise—agentic AI acts as a knowledge hub, providing instant access to quality management concepts, standards, and best practices.

4. Enhanced collaboration—AI facilitates seamless communication between team members, suppliers, and customers.

5. Cost efficiency—use of AI reduces the time and resources required for quality management activities, enabling leaner operations.

KEY STEPS FOR INTEGRATION

Successful integration of AI/ML relies on following these seven steps:

1. Define clear objectives.

   - Identify the specific quality management challenges you aim to address with AI/ML. For example, you may want to:
     - Reduce product defects by automating inspections.[13]
     - Enhance customer satisfaction through better complaint resolution.[14]
     - Improve process efficiency by predicting equipment failures.[15]

2. Assess current workflows.

   - Map existing QA/QC processes to identify inefficiencies and potential areas for AI/ML enhancement.

   - Understand data flows, decision points, and manual interventions that could benefit from automation or analysis.

3. Develop a proof of concept (PoC).

   - Start with a small-scale pilot project to test AI/ML capabilities in a controlled environment.

   - Use specific metrics (for example, defect detection accuracy, time savings) to evaluate success.

   - Example: Test a computer vision model on a single production line before scaling it across the factory.

4. Ensure data readiness.

   - Data collection: Gather high-quality data relevant to the chosen use case.

   - Data cleaning: Remove inconsistencies, duplicates, and errors.

   - Data labeling: Clearly label data for supervised learning tasks.

- Example: Label images as "defective" or "non-defective" for training an inspection model.

5. Collaborate across teams.

- Involve cross-functional teams (for example, quality assurance, information technology, and operations) to align AI/ML initiatives with organizational goals.

- Provide training to help team members understand how AI/ML enhances their roles.

6. Deploy AI/ML solutions gradually.

- Roll out solutions incrementally to manage risks and gather feedback.

- Integrate models into existing software systems or processes, such as enterprise resource planning (ERP) or manufacturing execution system (MES) platforms.

7. Monitor and optimize.

- Continuously evaluate the performance of AI/ML models using metrics like accuracy, precision, and ROI.

- Retrain models periodically with new data to ensure they remain effective as processes evolve.

OVERCOMING CHALLENGES

Not everyone will be ready for the digital transformation that AI brings. Challenges include:

1. Resistance to change

- Problem: Employees may fear job displacement or struggle to trust AI/ML outputs.

- Solutions:
  - Emphasize that AI/ML augments human capabilities rather than replacing them.
  - Provide training to build confidence in using AI/ML tools.

2. Data privacy and security
   - Problem: Handling sensitive data for AI/ML models raises privacy concerns.
   - Solutions:
     - Implement robust data encryption and access controls.
     - Ensure compliance with regulations like general data protection regulation (GDPR) or the Health Insurance Portability and Accountability Act (HIPAA).

3. Lack of technical expertise
   - Problem: Limited in-house AI/ML knowledge can hinder implementation.
   - Solutions:
     - Partner with AI/ML vendors or consultants.
     - Upskill existing staff through targeted training programs.

4. Integration complexity
   - Problem: Incorporating AI/ML into legacy systems can be challenging.
   - Solutions:
     - Use middleware or APIs to bridge gaps between new and existing technologies.
     - Gradually transition legacy systems to modern platforms that support AI/ML.

Conclusion: Driving Value Through Integration

Integrating AI/ML into quality workflows is a journey that requires careful planning, collaboration, and ongoing optimization. By starting small, addressing challenges proactively, and aligning initiatives with organizational goals, quality professionals can unlock the potential of AI/ML to enhance quality outcomes and drive business success. In the next chapter, we will explore how to measure the ROI of AI/ML initiatives in quality management.

Chapter 7
Measuring the ROI of AI/ML in Quality Management

Implementing AI and ML in quality can involve significant investment in time, resources, and infrastructure. To justify these investments, organizations must measure the return on investment (ROI) effectively. This chapter outlines how to evaluate the financial, operational, and strategic benefits of AI/ML.

ROI measures the benefits gained relative to the costs incurred. For AI/ML initiatives in quality management, these benefits can include:

1. Cost savings: Reductions in labor, rework, waste, and downtime.

2. Efficiency gains: Streamlined processes and faster decision-making.

3. Quality improvements: Reduced defect rates, higher customer satisfaction, and improved compliance.

4. Revenue growth: Increased production capacity, faster time to market, and enhanced product value.

STEPS TO MEASURE ROI

We should start by integrating the "quality cost" framework into ROI measurement. This ensures a comprehensive understanding of how AI/ML impacts the organization from a quality standpoint in words that are well understood by quality leadership. For example:

- Prevention costs are directly tied to the initial investment in AI/ML tools and training.

- Appraisal costs decrease as AI/ML improves defect detection accuracy and efficiency.

- Internal and external failure costs are minimized through predictive analytics and real-time monitoring.

To measure ROI:

1. Establish baseline metrics.

   - Identify current performance metrics to serve as benchmarks.
   - Examples include:
     - Average defect rate.
     - Cost of rework and scrap.
     - Production cycle times.
     - Customer complaint resolution time.

2. Define AI/ML objectives and expected outcomes.

   - Align objectives with business goals.
   - Examples:
     - Reduce defect rates by 20%.
     - Cut inspection time by half using automated visual inspections.
     - Improve customer complaint categorization accuracy to 95%.

3. Calculate costs.

   - Account for all costs associated with the AI/ML initiative. This includes:
     - Hardware and software investments
     - Data collection and preparation
     - Model development and training
     - Deployment and integration
     - Ongoing maintenance and retraining

4. Quantify benefits.

- Track improvements directly attributable to AI/ML implementation, such as:
  - A reduction in defect-related costs
  - Savings from predictive maintenance
  - Productivity gains from automated processes
  - Enhanced customer retention due to improved satisfaction

5. Compute ROI.

- Use the formula:

  ROI (%) = [(Benefits – Costs) / Costs] x 100

- Example:
  - Benefits: $200,000 saved from reduced defects.
  - Costs: $50,000 for AI/ML deployment.
  - ROI = [(200,000 – 50,000) / 50,000] x 100 = 300%.

ROI Examples

Real-world ROI analysis includes:

1. Automated visual inspection

- Scenario: A manufacturer implemented AI-powered computer vision to inspect products.[1]
- Benefits:
  - Inspection time was reduced by 60%, saving $100,000 annually in labor costs.
  - Defect detection accuracy improved from 85% to 98%, reducing rework costs by $50,000 annually.
- Costs: $75,000 for implementation and training
- ROI: 200%

2. Customer complaint analysis

- Scenario: An organization used ChatGPT to automate complaint categorization and response generation.[2]
- Benefits:
  - Resolution time was reduced by 50%, saving $80,000 annually in labor costs.
  - Customer satisfaction scores increased by 15%.
- Costs: $40,000 for API integration and fine-tuning
- ROI: 100%

Intangible Benefits

In addition to measurable financial gains, AI/ML delivers intangible benefits that support long-term success, such as:

1. Improved decision-making—real-time insights enable better strategic decisions.
2. Enhanced innovation—freeing up resources allows teams to focus on high-value activities.
3. Brand reputation—higher quality standards and faster response times improve customer perceptions.
4. Regulatory compliance—automated monitoring reduces the risk of compliance breaches.

Common pitfalls in measuring ROI include:

1. Ignoring indirect benefits: Overlooking downstream impacts, such as improved customer loyalty or employee productivity.
2. Underestimating costs: Failing to include ongoing costs like model retraining and system updates.
3. Short-term focus: Neglecting long-term gains like scalability and adaptability.
4. Data silos: Incomplete data integration can lead to inaccurate assessments.

Best practices for accurate ROI assessment include:

1. Use real-time metrics. Leverage dashboards to monitor AI/ML impact continuously.

2. Account for intangibles. Include qualitative benefits like customer satisfaction and employee engagement.

3. Iterate and refine. Adjust ROI calculations as new data become available.

4. Benchmark against industry standards. Compare ROI metrics with similar organizations to gauge effectiveness.

Conclusion: Demonstrating the Value of AI/ML in Quality Management

Measuring ROI is essential for justifying AI/ML investments and guiding future initiatives. By carefully and objectively quantifying costs and benefits, quality professionals can talk the language of business leaders and showcase the transformative value of these technologies. In the next chapter, we will explore how to foster a culture of AI-driven innovation within quality management teams and organizations.

Chapter 8

Leadership's Role in Fostering a Culture of AI Innovation

Introducing AI and ML into quality assurance (QA) and quality control (QC) is not just about adopting new tools—it's about cultivating a mindset of continuous improvement, innovation, and collaboration. Building a culture that embraces AI/ML requires leadership, education, and a strategic approach to change management. This chapter explores how organizations can foster such a culture to unlock the full potential of AI/ML technologies.

THE ROLE OF LEADERSHIP IN DRIVING AI/ML INNOVATION

Leaders should follow three important steps to facilitate successful AI-focused change:

1. Vision and advocacy

    - Articulate a clear vision for how AI/ML can enhance quality management.

    - Understand that advocacy and support from top management ensures alignment of AI/ML initiatives with organizational goals as they roll down through the organizational rungs.

2. Strategic investment

    - Allocate resources for AI/ML training, infrastructure, and pilot projects.

    - Commit to long-term investment, understanding that benefits may evolve over time.

3. Empowering teams

- Encourage teams to experiment with AI/ML applications and share successes.

- Foster an environment where it's safe to fail.

- Promote cross-functional collaboration to integrate diverse perspectives, especially since dealing with AI/ML is often considered a job for IT. Form teams with members from QA, operations, IT, and data science to develop AI/ML projects.

- Facilitate open communication channels between departments.

- Use collaborative platforms to share data, models, and insights.

BUILDING AI LITERACY

Enhance AI literacy across your organization with:

1. Tailored training programs

- Develop training modules that cater to different levels of expertise:
    - Introductory: Basics of AI/ML for non-technical staff to make them comfortable with the technology.
    - Intermediate: Hands-on workshops for operational teams for practical AI implementation.
    - Advanced: In-depth coding courses for data scientists and IT professionals.

2. Knowledge sharing

- Create forums for employees to discuss AI/ML use cases and lessons learned.

- Example: Host monthly lunch-and-learn sessions on emerging AI tools.

3. Gamification and incentives

- Use gamification to make learning about AI/ML engaging and fun.

- Recognize and reward employees who contribute innovative ideas using AI/ML.

CREATING AN ENVIRONMENT OF EXPERIMENTATION

Ensure your organization has the freedom to explore AI with confidence by adopting:

1. Pilot projects

   - Start with small-scale, low-risk projects to demonstrate quick wins.

   - Example: Use AI to optimize a single production line before scaling.

2. A safe-to-fail approach

   - Allow teams to experiment without fear of repercussions for failures.

   - Emphasize learning from mistakes as a pathway to innovation.

3. Continuous feedback loops

   - Implement mechanisms for gathering feedback on AI/ML deployments.

   - Regularly iterate and improve based on user input and results.

Overcome resistance to change by:

1. Addressing fears and automation anxiety

   - Leaders have to emphasize that AI/ML augments human roles rather than replacing them. A worker who knows AI will soon be more valuable than a worker who does not.

   - Managers should provide clear pathways for upskilling employees.

2. Offering transparent communication

- Leaders should explain the rationale behind AI/ML initiatives and their benefits, including cost-benefit ratios.
- Always celebrate success and share success stories to build trust and enthusiasm.

3. Planning gradual implementation

- Roll out AI/ML solutions incrementally, allowing time for adaptation.

BEST PRACTICES FOR SUSTAINING AI-DRIVEN INNOVATION

1. Celebrate success. Publicly recognize teams and individuals who drive successful AI/ML initiatives.

2. Institutionalize learning. Document and share AI/ML implementation strategies and lessons learned.

3. Stay future-focused. Continuously monitor advancements in AI/ML and adapt strategies to leverage new opportunities.

Conclusion: Transforming Culture, Unlocking Potential

Fostering a culture of AI-driven innovation is essential for leveraging the full potential of AI/ML in quality management. By prioritizing leadership, collaboration, and continuous learning, organizations can position themselves at the forefront of technological advancement.

Chapter 9

Data as the Cornerstone of Quality

Data make up the backbone of every successful quality management strategy, particularly in the realm of AI and ML. High-quality data empower organizations to make accurate predictions, derive actionable insights, and drive continuous improvement. However, the journey from raw data to meaningful results involves careful collection, cleaning, and maintenance. This chapter delves into the best practices for managing data and ensuring their integrity and reliability for AI/ML applications (Figure 9.1).

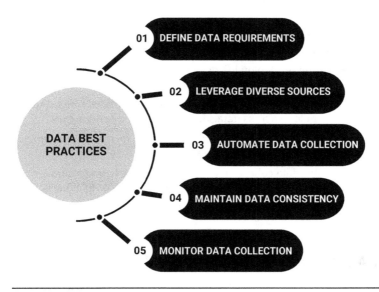

Figure 9.1 Best practices for data collection.

COLLECTING QUALITY DATA: BEST PRACTICES

The success of AI/ML models hinges on the quality of data on which they are trained. Here are best practices for collecting data that meet the high standards required for quality management:

1. Define data requirements. Clearly outline the goals of the AI/ML initiative and the type of data needed to achieve them.

   - Example: For predictive maintenance, collect sensor data such as temperature, vibration, and runtime hours.

2. Leverage diverse data sources. Combine data from multiple sources, such as production logs, customer feedback, and IoT devices.

   - Ensure all sources contribute to a comprehensive view of quality metrics.

3. Automate data collection. Use sensors, software integrations, and automated tools to minimize human errors and ensure real-time data availability.

   - Example: Deploy IoT devices on production lines to continuously capture machine performance data.

4. Maintain data consistency. Standardize formats, units, and terminology across data sources to avoid discrepancies.

   - Example: Use a consistent timestamp format (for example, ISO 8601) for all collected data.

5. Monitor data collection processes. Regularly audit data collection methods to ensure accuracy and completeness.

   - Implement checks to detect gaps or anomalies in incoming data.

DATA CLEANING AND PREPROCESSING FOR AI/ML

Raw data often contain errors, inconsistencies, and noise that can compromise AI/ML model performance. Cleaning and preprocessing transform these raw data into a format suitable for analysis and modeling.

1. Handle missing data.

   - Identify and address missing values:
     - Imputation: Replace missing values with averages, medians, or predictions.
     - Removal: Discard incomplete records if they are non-critical.

2. Remove duplicates.

   - Ensure that data records are unique to avoid biasing the model with redundant entries.
   - Example: De-duplicate customer feedback entries before sentiment analysis.[1]

3. Normalize and scale data.

   - Standardize numeric data to ensure uniformity:
     - Normalization: Scale data to a range of 0-1.
     - Standardization: Adjust data to have a mean of 0 and a standard deviation of 1.
   - Example: Normalize sensor readings for consistent analysis across machines.[2]

4. Detect and address outliers.

   - Use statistical methods or visualization tools to identify outliers.
   - Decide whether to remove, adjust, or flag outliers based on their relevance.

5. Encode categorical data.

   - Convert text-based data into numerical formats suitable for AI/ML models:
     - One-hot encoding: Create binary columns for each category.
     - Label encoding: Assign numerical values to categories.

6. Validate data quality.

- Use tools to check for:
  - Completeness: Are all necessary fields populated?
  - Accuracy: Do the data align with known values or ranges?
  - Consistency: Are there conflicts between data sources?

ENSURING DATA INTEGRITY AND RELIABILITY

For AI/ML to deliver meaningful insights, data integrity and reliability must be maintained throughout its life cycle. Follow the steps below:

1. Implement data governance policies.

- Define roles, responsibilities, and processes for managing data.
- Example: Assign a data steward to oversee data quality initiatives.

2. Use robust data storage solutions.

- Store data in secure, scalable systems that support real-time access.
- Example: Use cloud platforms with built-in data validation features.[3]

3. Secure data from breaches.

- Encrypt sensitive data and restrict access based on user roles.
- Ensure compliance with regulations like GDPR or HIPAA.

4. Perform regular data audits.

- Periodically review datasets for accuracy, completeness, and relevance.
- Example: Audit production data monthly to ensure alignment with quality standards.[4]

5. Monitor data drift.

   - Detect shifts in data patterns over time that could degrade AI/ML model performance.
   - Example: Monitor changes in customer behavior data and update models accordingly.[5]

6. Foster a culture of data accuracy.

   - Train employees on the importance of accurate data entry and adherence to data policies.
   - Provide tools and incentives to encourage diligent data management.

CASE STUDY: DATA PREPARATION FOR PREDICTIVE MAINTENANCE

Scenario: A manufacturing company wants to implement predictive maintenance using ML models trained on equipment sensor data.

Steps taken:

1. Data collection

   - Installed IoT sensors on critical machinery to gather temperature, pressure, and vibration data.

2. Data cleaning

   - Removed duplicate records caused by sensor malfunctions.
   - Imputed missing data points using historical averages.

3. Data preprocessing

   - Normalized sensor readings to ensure uniformity.
   - Flagged and analyzed outliers to identify potential equipment anomalies.

4. Ensuring integrity

   - Stored data in a centralized, cloud-based system with real-time validation checks.

Outcome: The company achieved a 30% reduction in unplanned downtime by leveraging clean, reliable data to train accurate predictive models.

Conclusion: Building a Strong Data Foundation

High-quality data are essential for effective quality management and AI/ML initiatives. By following best practices for data collection, cleaning, and integrity, organizations can ensure their AI/ML models deliver accurate, actionable insights. In the next chapter, we will explore how real-time analytics can transform decision-making in quality management.

Chapter 10
Predictive Quality Analytics

Predictive analytics is revolutionizing quality management by enabling organizations to anticipate defects, failures, and other quality-related issues before they occur. Leveraging AI and ML, predictive analytics provides actionable insights, enhancing proactive decision-making and reducing costs associated with reactive measures. This chapter introduces predictive analytics, explains its application in forecasting defects and failures, and showcases real-world case studies that demonstrate its effectiveness.

INTRODUCTION TO PREDICTIVE ANALYTICS

Predictive analytics involves analyzing historical and real-time data to predict future outcomes. In quality management, predictive models identify patterns, trends, and anomalies, empowering teams to address potential issues proactively.

Predictive analytics is a transformative discipline at the intersection of statistical modeling, machine learning, and data science, aimed at forecasting future outcomes based on historical and real-time data. It serves as a cornerstone in the broader realm of AI and is pivotal in domains ranging from healthcare and finance to manufacturing and quality assurance. By leveraging sophisticated algorithms and computational techniques, predictive analytics enables the identification of patterns, trends, and relationships in large and complex datasets, driving actionable insights and data-informed decision-making.

Predictive analytics is concerned with estimating the likelihood of future events or behaviors. It employs a variety of methodologies, including regression analysis, decision trees, ensemble methods, neural networks, and support vector machines, to develop predictive models.

These models are trained on historical data, where relationships between input variables (features) and outcomes (targets) are learned. Once trained, these models can generalize to unseen data, providing probabilistic or deterministic predictions.

The technical underpinnings of predictive analytics rely on several fundamental components, as shown in Figure 10.1. We will elaborate on this with a focus on quality in the next section.

Predictive analytics transcends traditional descriptive analysis by not only summarizing historical data but also uncovering latent patterns that signal future behaviors. The convergence of computational power, big data, and advanced algorithms has exponentially enhanced its capabilities. Today, predictive analytics is integral to applications such as personalized medicine, fraud detection, demand forecasting, predictive maintenance, and customer segmentation.

From a theoretical perspective, predictive analytics draws heavily on principles from probability theory, optimization, and information theory. The probabilistic frameworks underpinning Bayesian inference and Markov models offer mechanisms for incorporating uncertainty and dynamic systems into predictions. Additionally, advancements in reinforcement learning and transfer learning further enhance predictive systems' adaptability to evolving environments.

KEY COMPONENTS OF PREDICTIVE ANALYTICS FOR QUALITY

The goal of predictive analytics is to transform raw data into actionable insights so that organizations can move from a reactive to proactive approach to quality decision making. The effectiveness of predictive analytics for quality lies in its structured approach, which involves data collection, preprocessing, modeling, validation, and continuous improvement. Let us expand on these key critical components in this section.

1. Data collection and preparation: Gather historical and real-time data from sources such as production logs, sensor readings, and customer feedback.

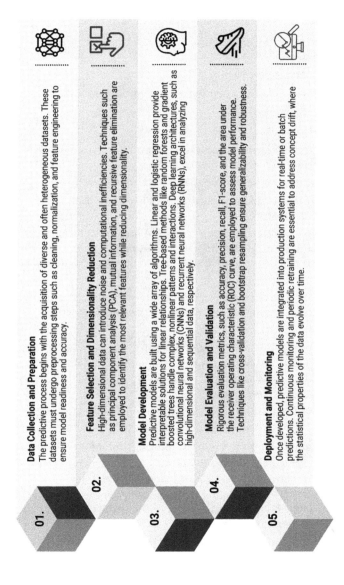

Data Collection and Preparation

The predictive process begins with the acquisition of diverse and often heterogeneous datasets. These datasets must undergo preprocessing steps such as cleaning, normalization, and feature engineering to ensure model readiness and accuracy.

Feature Selection and Dimensionality Reduction

High-dimensional data can introduce noise and computational inefficiencies. Techniques such as principal component analysis (PCA), mutual information, and recursive feature elimination are employed to identify the most relevant features while reducing dimensionality.

Model Development

Predictive models are built using a wide array of algorithms. Linear and logistic regression provide interpretable solutions for linear relationships. Tree-based methods like random forests and gradient boosted trees handle complex, nonlinear patterns and interactions. Deep learning architectures, such as convolutional neural networks (CNNs) and recurrent neural networks (RNNs), excel in analyzing high-dimensional and sequential data, respectively.

Model Evaluation and Validation

Rigorous evaluation metrics, such as accuracy, precision, recall, F1-score, and the area under the receiver operating characteristic (ROC) curve, are employed to assess model performance. Techniques like cross-validation and bootstrap resampling ensure generalizability and robustness.

Deployment and Monitoring

Once developed, predictive models are integrated into production systems for real-time or batch predictions. Continuous monitoring and periodic retraining are essential to address concept drift, where the statistical properties of the data evolve over time.

Figure 10.1 Fundamental concepts and the life cycle of predictive modeling.

Identify relevant data sources:

- Production records
- Quality control reports
- Customer feedback
- Sensor data from manufacturing equipment
- Maintenance logs

Data cleaning and pre-processing:

- Handle missing values using imputation (mean/mode/median replacement) or deletion.
- Remove outliers through statistical or ML techniques.
- Normalize and standardize data to ensure uniformity across features.
- Convert categorical variables into numerical formats using encoding techniques (for example, one-hot encoding and label encoding). Handle missing values (imputation or deletion).

2. Feature selection and dimensionality reduction: Efficiently reduce data complexity to focus on the most impactful predictors.

   - Identify and retain relevant features using:
     - Statistical tests such as Chi-square or ANOVA.
     - Recursive feature elimination (RFE) to iteratively rank feature importance.
     - Mutual information or correlation analysis to identify dependencies.
   - Simplify datasets while retaining critical information using:
     - Principal component analysis (PCA), which reduces features to uncorrelated principal components.
     - t-SNE (t-distributed stochastic neighbor embedding), which visualizes high-dimensional data in lower dimensions.
     - Autoencoders, or neural network-based compression techniques.

3. Model development: Use ML algorithms to identify correlations and make predictions.

   Choose appropriate models:

   - Regression models (linear, logistic, or polynomial)
   - Time series models (ARIMA or exponential smoothing)
   - Machine learning algorithms (decision trees, random forests, support vector machines, or neural networks)

   Train and validate models:

   - Split data into training and testing sets.
   - Train models on training data.
   - Evaluate model performance on testing data using metrics like accuracy, precision, recall, F1-score, and mean-squared error.

4. Implementation: Integrate predictive insights into quality workflows for real-time decision-making.

   Integrate models into QA/QC systems:

   - Deploy models as APIs or web services.
   - Integrate with existing QA/QC software.

   Monitor model performance:

   - Track model accuracy and precision over time.
   - Retrain models as needed to adapt to changing conditions.
   - Implement alert systems to notify stakeholders of potential issues.

5. Continuous improvement: Monitor and refine models to adapt to changing conditions.

Benefits to Quality Management

Predictive analytics for quality is a highly technical strategic approach that harnesses data, advanced statistical techniques, and machine learning algorithms to forecast quality outcomes and proactively address potential issues. This forward-looking methodology enables organizations to move from a reactive stance to a proactive quality management strategy, offering several key benefits:

- Proactive issue resolution: Detect potential defects or failures before they escalate.
- Cost reduction: Minimize waste, rework, and warranty claims by addressing issues early.
- Improved customer satisfaction: Deliver consistent product quality by preventing defects.
- Efficiency gains: Optimize production processes through data-driven adjustments.

USE CASES FOR PREDICTIVE ANALYTICS IN QUALITY

1. Defect prediction
   - How it works:
     - Analyze production data to identify variables contributing to defects.
     - Train ML models on historical defect patterns.
   - Example: A car manufacturer uses predictive analytics to identify paint defects caused by humidity changes in the painting booth.[1]

2. Equipment failure prediction and predictive maintenance
   - How it works:
     - Use IoT sensors to collect equipment performance data (for example, vibration, temperature).
     - Train models to recognize early warning signs of equipment failure.
   - Example: A factory predicts bearing failures in assembly line machinery, enabling timely maintenance and avoiding downtime.[2]

3. Process optimization
   - How it works:
     - Continuously analyze production data to identify inefficiencies.

    - Adjust processes in real time to maintain optimal
      performance.
  - Example: A pharmaceutical company adjusts mixing
    times and temperatures during production to ensure batch
    consistency.[3]

4. Anomaly detection

  - How it works:
    - Use unsupervised learning models to detect deviations
      from normal operating conditions.
    - Flag anomalies for investigation.
  - Example: A food processing plant identifies unexpected
    temperature fluctuations in storage units, preventing
    spoilage.[4]

CASE STUDIES: USING AI FOR PROACTIVE QUALITY ASSURANCE

Case Study 1: Predictive Analytics in Electronics Manufacturing

- Scenario: A semiconductor manufacturer faced persistent high
  defect rates in microchip production, leading to substantial
  rework costs and delays in meeting delivery schedules.
  Traditional quality checks were time-consuming and often
  identified issues only after they had escalated.

- Solutions:
  - The company deployed predictive analytics to analyze
    vast amounts of production data, including variables
    such as machine temperature, humidity, operator shift
    patterns, and material batch properties. Using advanced
    ML algorithms, they developed a defect prediction model
    that could identify the most influential factors contributing
    to defects.
  - Additionally, IoT sensors were installed on critical
    equipment to provide real-time data inputs for the model.
    This integration allowed the system to continuously

monitor conditions and issue alerts whenever parameters approached thresholds linked to higher defect rates.[5]

- Implementation steps:

1. Data collection
   - Historical production data spanning two years were consolidated into a centralized database.
   - Real-time data streams from IoT sensors were integrated for dynamic analysis.

2. Model training: ML algorithms were trained on historical defect data to identify patterns and correlations.

3. Deployment: The trained model was deployed onto the production floor and integrated with existing quality management software.

4. Validation and optimization: Predictions were validated against actual production outcomes, and the model was fine-tuned for higher accuracy.

- Outcomes:

   - Defect rates decreased by 25% within six months, resulting in direct savings of over $2 million annually in rework and scrap costs.

   - Production throughput improved by 15% as fewer defective batches required stoppages for correction.

   - The company also gained valuable insights into optimizing environmental conditions and raw material sourcing, further reducing variability in quality outcomes.

Case Study 2: Preventing Equipment Failures in Heavy Machinery

- Scenario: A mining company operating in remote locations experienced frequent equipment breakdowns, leading to costly unplanned downtime and disruptions in production schedules. These failures not only increased maintenance costs but also caused cascading delays across logistics and supply chain operations.

- Solution:
  - The company implemented a predictive maintenance solution powered by IoT sensors and AI-driven analytics. IoT devices were installed on critical machinery, such as haul trucks, conveyor belts, and crushers, to continuously monitor performance metrics like vibration, temperature, pressure, and oil viscosity. The data collected were fed into a ML model trained on historical failure data to identify early warning signs of potential breakdowns.
- Implementation steps:
  1. Data collection
     - IoT sensors transmitted real-time performance data to a centralized cloud platform.
     - Historical maintenance logs were digitized and used to train the predictive model.
  2. Model training: ML algorithms were trained to recognize patterns associated with failures, such as abnormal vibration levels or temperature spikes.
  3. Integration with maintenance systems: The predictive model was integrated with the company's existing maintenance management software, triggering automated alerts when anomalies were detected.
  4. Maintenance optimization: Schedules were adjusted based on predictions, prioritizing equipment at higher risk of failure.
- Outcomes:
  - The predictive maintenance system reduced unplanned downtime by 40%, saving an estimated $5 million annually in production losses.
  - Equipment lifespan was extended by 20% due to timely interventions, reducing capital expenditure on new machinery.

- The solution also improved worker safety by preventing catastrophic failures and ensuring the equipment operated within safe parameters.

- Over time, the company's predictive model accuracy improved as more data were collected, enhancing its reliability and further minimizing disruptions.

BEST PRACTICES FOR IMPLEMENTING PREDICTIVE ANALYTICS

When implementing predictive analytics:

1. Start with high-value use cases. Focus on areas where predictions can significantly impact costs or customer satisfaction.

2. Invest in data quality. Ensure data are accurate, complete, and representative of real-world conditions.

3. Collaborate across teams. Involve QA, operations, and IT teams to align objectives and resources.

4. Monitor and update models. Evaluate model performance continuously and retrain with updated data to maintain accuracy.

5. Leverage scalable tools. Use cloud-based AI platforms to scale predictive analytics across multiple processes or locations.

Conclusion: The Power of Prediction

Predictive analytics enables organizations to move beyond reactive quality management, empowering them to anticipate and address issues before they occur. By leveraging AI/ML technologies, companies can achieve significant cost savings, efficiency gains, and customer satisfaction improvements.

Chapter 11

AI for Root Cause Analysis and Non-Conformance Management

Management of non-conformances and root cause analysis (RCA) are critical in any quality management system. This is a mostly manual process that requires a lot of cross-functional human resources. With AI as an assistant, this highly creative and generative activity can get a kickstart, and quality professionals can level continually with AI recommendations to ensure they have covered all the bases in an investigation. Advanced AI integrations, such as those with IoTs on production lines, can further hasten RCA by analyzing generated production data and identifying patterns and issues. This chapter explores how AI enhances RCA, automates non-conformance tracking, and leverages trend analysis to drive continuous improvement.

AUTOMATING ROOT CAUSE IDENTIFICATION WITH AI

RCA is a creative brainstorming exercise that involves identifying the underlying causes of failures, issues, or risks. Traditionally, RCA relies on manual investigation methods such as fishbone diagrams, 5 Whys analysis, and brainstorming sessions. AI, however, can automate and enhance RCA by analyzing data at scale and identifying patterns that may elude human detection. AI can also act as an assistant to the investigator and propose multiple root cause theories and automatically fill out the investigator's tool of choice.

DO IT YOURSELF

The prompt in Figure 11.1 was provided to ChatGPT-4o. Try this yourself by providing any quality issue to the free ChatGPT AI agent and asking for a structured root cause analysis using the method of your choice.

do a fish bone root cause analysis of spinal pedicle screw implant failure at L5. The implant returned by the hospital showed ductile fracture.

‹ 2/2 ›

Figure 11.1 RCA ChatGPT prompt.

The output is shown in Figure 11.2.

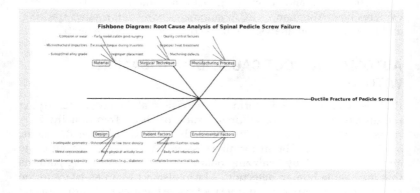

Figure 11.2 ChatGPT RCA output.

Additionally, the AI provided a lot of commentary on the cause. While this is not perfect and very broad, it gives the investigator a great starting point.

The more information you provide (the more prompt engineering you do), the more targeted the RCA will become. In this case, I just provided very basic and general information, and yet GPT was able give back something usable that would be great seeding material for an RCA team. AI, when asked, can also do the following:

1. Simulated scenarios

   - AI simulates various scenarios to test potential causes and validate hypotheses.
   - Example: Testing different raw material sources to determine their impact on defect rates.

2. Natural language processing (NLP)

   - AI processes unstructured data, such as operator notes or maintenance logs, complaints, and customer feedback, to extract insights and link them to recurring issues.
   - Example: Analyzing maintenance records to discover a pattern of late calibrations contributing to failures.

ADVANCED RCA FOR CONNECTED AI

If AI is connected to your enterprise resource planning (ERP) systems or part of your inspection systems like vision detection, then you can leverage it to collate data and mine it for root causes. There are two ways AI can help RCA in advanced cases.

Causal inference: AI can use causal inference techniques to determine the true cause-and-effect relationships between variables, helping to distinguish between correlation and causation. This requires us to feed the AI a large amount of data, define parameters of interest, and have it perform mining operations.

Rule-based systems: AI-powered rule-based systems can be designed to apply specific rules and logic to identify potential root causes based on predefined criteria. This is possible without a large amount of data, but it requires pre-work in informing the knowledge base of the AI model. This will require creation of a bespoke pretrained model such as My GPT in OpenAI or the agent in Copilot Studio, as shown in Chapter 4.

There are four components of a rule-based system:

1. Knowledge base

   - It contains a set of rules and facts that represent domain knowledge.

- Rules are often written as *IF (condition) THEN (action/ conclusion)*.

2. Inference engine
   - It is the reasoning mechanism that applies the rules to input data to derive conclusions.
   - It evaluates which rules are satisfied and determines the appropriate actions or outputs.
   - It can use strategies like forward chaining (data-driven) or backward chaining (goal-driven).

3. Working memory
   - This is temporary data storage that keeps track of facts or inputs provided to the system during execution.

4. User interface
   - This allows users to input data, interact with the system, and receive outputs.

In advanced cases, where AI is part of production systems and using causal inference or rule-based systems, it can perform:

- Data integration and analysis
  - AI can integrate data from multiple sources (for example, production logs, equipment sensors, and customer complaints) to provide a comprehensive view of the issue.
  - Example: A manufacturer uses AI to analyze sensor data and identifies that temperature fluctuations during assembly cause defects.

- Pattern recognition
  - ML algorithms detect correlations and anomalies in data that point to potential root causes.
  - Example: AI flags a specific machine in a production line as the source of frequent defects based on historical performance data.

AI-DRIVEN NON-CONFORMANCE REPORTING AND TRACKING

Non-conformance management involves documenting, tracking, and resolving deviations from quality standards where an item under study fails to meet specified requirements. AI can greatly streamline this process, ensuring timely responses and preventing recurring issues. The following example shows how fast AI can be in generating first drafts of reports, even based on minimal information. These won't be 100% accurate, but the investigator is now focused on polishing the report, adding and removing items from it rather than starting from scratch. Two features of AI-based non-conformance systems are to be noted:

1. Automated report generation and reporting

   - AI generates fast non-conformance reports based on data inputs, eliminating the need for onerous administrative documentation.

   - In an advanced system, it is possible for AI to detect a non-conformance and then generate a report itself – for example, a system may automatically create a report when a sensor detects a temperature reading outside of the control range.

2. Prioritization and escalation

   - If taught the rule, AI can automatically rank non-conformance issues based on severity, impact, and recurrence, ensuring critical problems are addressed first.

   - Example: A repeated deviation in pharmaceutical production is escalated to senior management for immediate action.

DO IT YOURSELF

The prompt shown in Figure 11.3 was given to ChatGPT, and within 30 seconds it was able to write a non-conformance report (NCR), as shown in the next section.

Figure 11.3   Non-conformance ChatGPT prompt.

Output of ChatGPT:

Non-Conformance Report (NCR)

Report ID: NCR-2024-001

Date: [Insert Date]

Reported By: [Insert Name/Department]

Product: Pedicle Screw (Part ID: PS-L5-001)

Location: [Manufacturing Facility Name/Location]

---

1. Description of Non-Conformance

*A pedicle screw was found to deviate from the specified dimension. The screw was manufactured with a **diameter exceeding the specification by 0.005mm**. The allowable tolerance for the screw diameter is **[Insert Range, e.g., ± 0.002mm]**. The non-conformance was identified during routine quality inspection using precision measuring tools (e.g., micrometer or laser measurement system).*

---

2. Non-Conformance Details

- ***Specification:** [Insert Correct Specification, e.g., 5.000mm ± 0.002mm]*
- ***Measured Value:** 5.005mm*
- ***Deviation:** +0.005mm*

- *Quantity Affected:* [Insert Quantity, e.g., 5 units]
- *Detection Method:* Routine inspection after manufacturing
- *Impact:* Potential risk of improper fit, decreased stability, and increased patient safety concerns if used in spinal surgery.

3. Root Cause Analysis

Likely Cause: Lathe Machine Error

- Possible factors contributing to this error:
  - Incorrect machine calibration.
  - Tool wear or improper cutting tool alignment.
  - Vibration or instability during the machining process.
  - Insufficient machine maintenance.

Supporting Evidence:

- Machine calibration records and tool inspection logs are being reviewed to confirm the cause.

4. Containment Actions

Immediate actions taken to address the non-conformance:

1. *Isolation:* The affected screws have been quarantined to prevent further use.
2. *Production Hold:* Lathe machine operations have been temporarily halted for reinspection.
3. *Inspection Expansion:* 100% inspection of all screws produced in the affected batch.
4. *Notification:* Quality Assurance (QA) and Manufacturing departments have been notified.

5. Corrective Actions

- *Action 1:* Recalibrate the lathe machine and verify settings against standard specifications.

- **Action 2:** *Replace or regrind cutting tools if wear is identified.*
- **Action 3:** *Implement additional inline dimensional checks for pedicle screws during machining.*
- **Action 4:** *Conduct training for machine operators on machine calibration and tool maintenance procedures.*

6. Preventive Actions

- *Develop a preventive maintenance schedule for lathe machines.*
- *Integrate an automated machine monitoring system to detect calibration or alignment deviations in real-time.*
- *Enhance statistical process control (SPC) to track deviations during production.*
- *Conduct periodic audits of all measuring equipment used for critical dimensions.*

7. Verification of Corrective Actions

- *A retest of the lathe machine will be performed to ensure dimensional accuracy.*
- *Post-correction, a sample batch of screws will undergo full dimensional analysis.*
- *Follow-up inspections will ensure compliance with specification limits.*

8. Approval

- **Prepared By:** *[Insert Name, Title, Department]*
- **Reviewed By:** *[Insert QA Manager/Quality Engineer Name]*
- *Approved By: [Insert Quality Director or Authorized Personnel Name]*

Attachments

1. **Dimensional Inspection Report** *(pre- and post-correction)*
2. **Calibration Records** *of the lathe machine*

3. *Tool Wear Analysis Report*

4. *Batch Production Record*

End of Report

This report ensures that the root cause is identified, containment actions are implemented immediately, and both corrective and preventive actions are clearly outlined to prevent recurrence.

TREND ANALYSIS TO PREVENT RECURRING ISSUES

AI excels at identifying patterns and trends in quality data, enabling organizations to proactively address issues before they recur. In advanced systems where AI has access to NC repositories and other organizational data lakes, predictive insights can be gained using the sequential process below.

Steps in AI-powered trend analysis:

1. Data aggregation
   - AI consolidates data from various systems, such as ERP, MES, and QMS platforms, into a unified dataset.

2. Historical analysis
   - ML models analyze historical data to uncover recurring patterns.
   - Example: Identifying that defects increase during certain shifts due to staffing changes.

3. Real-time monitoring
   - AI continuously monitors data streams to detect emerging trends.
   - Example: Spotting a gradual rise in equipment vibration levels indicating impending failure.

4. Predictive insights
   - AI predicts future trends based on historical and real-time data, allowing proactive interventions.

- Example: Forecasting that a specific batch of raw materials is likely to result in higher defect rates based on past performance.

5. Actionable recommendations

   - AI provides actionable insights to prevent recurring issues.

   - Example: Recommending process adjustments or supplier changes based on identified trends.

ADVANCED CASE STUDY: AI-ENHANCED NON-CONFORMANCE MANAGEMENT

Scenario: A medical device manufacturer struggled with recurring non-conformance issues during assembly, leading to delays in shipments and regulatory risks.

Solutions:

1. Automated RCA: AI analyzed sensor data from assembly lines and identified a specific calibration error in one machine as the cause.

2. Non-conformance tracking: An AI-driven system documented all deviations, prioritized issues based on impact, and escalated critical cases to quality managers.

3. Trend analysis: ML models revealed a correlation between increased defects and operator shift changes, prompting process standardization during transitions.

4. Preventive actions: AI recommended a recalibration schedule for the machine and improved training for operators during shift handovers.

Outcomes:

- Non-conformance events were reduced by 40% within six months.

- On-time shipment rates improved by 25%.

- Compliance with regulatory standards was enhanced, avoiding potential penalties.

Conclusion: Transforming Non-Conformance Management with AI

AI-powered tools for RCA and non-conformance management enable organizations to address quality issues efficiently and proactively. By automating reporting, tracking, and trend analysis, AI reduces human effort, minimizes recurring problems, and ensures compliance with quality standards.

Chapter 12
Machine Learning in Visual Inspection

Inspection and testing are crucial to ensuring product quality, but traditional methods can be time-consuming, inconsistent, and prone to human error. ML can enhance these processes by leveraging data-driven insights, automating visual inspections, and enabling adaptive testing strategies. This chapter explores how ML transforms inspection and testing, focusing on computer vision, accuracy improvements, and adaptive methods. See Appendices B and C for examples of vision-based inspection.

USING COMPUTER VISION FOR AUTOMATED INSPECTIONS

Computer vision, powered by ML algorithms, enables automated inspection systems to identify defects, anomalies, or inconsistencies with greater precision and speed than manual methods. OpenCV (Open Computer Vision Library) is widely used for inspection cameras on production lines to automate quality control processes, detect defects, and ensure product compliance. Its computer vision algorithms and tools allow for real-time image analysis, and it can be integrated with cameras and processing systems to perform tasks such as defect detection, dimensional measurements, object recognition, and classification.

Implementation of computer vision can involve the following steps:

1. Image acquisition

    - Cameras capture images or video of products on the production line.
    - Cameras can include high-resolution industrial cameras or specialized systems, such as thermal or infrared cameras.

2. Preprocessing

   - Images are preprocessed to improve clarity and remove noise such as:
     - Gray-scaling for simplicity.
     - Filtering (for example, Gaussian blur) to smooth images.
     - Thresholding to segment objects from the background.

3. Feature extraction and analysis

   - OpenCV algorithms extract features such as edges, shapes, textures, or colors.
   - Techniques like contour detection, morphological operations, and histogram analysis are applied.

4. Defect identification

   - The features are compared against predefined thresholds or templates.
   - Deviations are flagged as defects.

5. Integration with production line systems

   - OpenCV processes are integrated into automation systems, such as programmable logic controllers (PLCs) or robotics, to trigger actions. That may mean:
     - Rejecting defective items using robotic arms.
     - Alerting operators through alarms or visual signals.

Application of AI in this space can go into many details that would require a lot of human resources. A few examples are detailed below.

1. Defect detection. AI, using libraries like OpenCV, identifies defects like scratches, cracks, dents, missing components, or surface irregularities by analyzing images or video feeds from inspection cameras.

   - Examples:
     - Using edge detection (for example, Canny Edge Detector) to identify cracks in metal surfaces.

- Thresholding and contour analysis to detect missing screws or alignment issues in assembled products.

2. Surface inspection

- Detect imperfections in textures, such as color inconsistencies, stains, or roughness.
- Use image filtering techniques such as Gaussian Blur and template matching to identify deviations from an ideal product surface.
- Example: Inspection of polished materials, food packaging, or textile surfaces for uniformity.

3. Object detection and counting. Real-time detection and counting of objects on production lines using techniques like Hough transform, contours, and blob detection.

- Examples:
  - Detecting and counting bottles on a conveyor belt to ensure correct batch sizes.
  - Verifying that the required number of components are present in an assembly.

4. Dimensional measurement. AI may measure the dimensions of objects by analyzing images from calibrated cameras.

- Examples:
  - Verifying that screws or bolts meet required diameters and lengths using calibrated pixel-to-mm conversions.
  - Detecting deviations in product dimensions using image contours or geometric shape fitting.

5. Pattern matching and alignment. Template matching can be used to identify and verify patterns on products.

- Examples:
  - Ensuring labels, logos, or prints are placed correctly on packaging.
  - Detecting misalignment of components in electronic boards.

6. Color inspection. Color space transformations—such as blue, green, red (BGR) to hue, saturation, value (HSV)—to analyze and validate color consistency.

   - Examples:
     - Inspecting food items to ensure ripeness based on color.
     - Validating the color of painted or coated surfaces to match specifications.

7. Barcode and QR code detection. Integration with barcode and QR code decoding libraries to verify product labeling and traceability.

   - Example: Scanning barcodes to ensure correct product identification before shipment.

8. Motion analysis. Tracking of object movement on the production line to identify anomalies like blockages, delays, or erratic movements.

   - Example: Detecting bottlenecks in conveyor systems through optical flow analysis.

Advantages of computer vision include:

- Speed—AI/ML-based vision systems can process thousands of images in seconds, ensuring rapid inspections.

- Accuracy—AI/ML can reduce false positives and missed defects by recognizing patterns beyond human capability. Human vision is often hampered by light, angle of view, etc.

- Scalability—AI/ML can handle high-volume production environments for multiple parts effectively, only limited by the speed of computing that can be adjusted or increased.

CASE STUDY: AI-POWERED INSPECTION IN AUTOMOTIVE MANUFACTURING

Scenario: An automotive parts supplier faced challenges with inconsistent quality inspections for brake pads, resulting in increased defect rates and customer complaints.

Solutions:[1]

1. Implementation of computer vision
   - The supplier installed high-resolution cameras on inspection lines.
   - ML models were trained to detect cracks, uneven surfaces, and material inconsistencies.

2. Integration with testing systems
   - Inspection data and performance testing results were combined to correlate visual defects with functional failures.

3. Adaptive testing strategy
   - The supplier adjusted testing parameters dynamically based on defect patterns identified by the ML system.

Outcomes:

- Defect rates decreased by 35% within the first year of implementation.
- There was a 50% reduction in inspection time, improving throughput.
- Customer satisfaction scores increased due to consistent product quality.

Conclusion: Transforming Quality Assurance with ML

ML has the potential to revolutionize inspection and testing by enhancing speed, accuracy, and adaptability. From automated visual inspections to adaptive testing strategies, ML can empower organizations to maintain high standards while optimizing for costs and efficiency. In next chapter, let's take this idea to the next level and explore process optimization using AI.

Chapter 13
Process Optimization and Lean AI

Process optimization has always been at the heart of quality and operational excellence. Lean principles and Six Sigma methodologies provide structured frameworks to eliminate waste and reduce variability. When combined with AI and ML, these approaches evolve into powerful tools for dynamic and data-driven process improvement. This chapter explores how AI identifies bottlenecks, enhances lean and Six Sigma initiatives, and assists in value stream mapping.

Process optimization entails reduction of waste, elimination of defects, and reduction of delays—all of which AI is well-primed to do. Let us rehash how AI can help in identification and reduction of process bottlenecks.

USING AI TO IDENTIFY BOTTLENECKS IN PROCESSES

AI excels at analyzing complex processes to uncover inefficiencies and bottlenecks that impede productivity and quality. This includes:

1. Real-time data analysis

   - AI processes data from IoT sensors, production logs, and workflow software to identify delays or inefficiencies in real time.

   - Example: AI flags prolonged idle times on a packaging line, indicating a machine setup issue.[1]

2. Workflow mapping and simulation:

   - ML algorithms model workflows and simulate various scenarios to highlight areas for improvement.

- Example: An AI system simulates production schedules to determine the impact of resource allocation changes on throughput.[2]

3. Pattern recognition
   - AI identifies recurring patterns of inefficiency, such as delays caused by specific machines or operators.
   - Example: Analyzing data from a logistics operation, AI detects that loading delays frequently occur during peak hours.[3]

4. Predictive insights
   - By forecasting potential bottlenecks, AI enables proactive adjustments to prevent disruptions.
   - Example: AI predicts increased downtime for a machine nearing its maintenance threshold.[4]

ENHANCING LEAN AND SIX SIGMA INITIATIVES WITH ML

Lean and Six Sigma (LSS) aim to improve efficiency and quality by reducing waste and variability. ML takes these methodologies to the next level by automating analysis and providing predictive capabilities. The impact of AI on each LSS parameter is shown in Table 13.1.

VALUE STREAM MAPPING WITH AI-DRIVEN INSIGHTS

Value stream mapping (VSM) is a lean tool used to visualize the current state of a process and design an improved future state by identifying waste, inefficiencies, and opportunities for improvement. It maps every step in a process, whether value-added or non-value-added, to optimize flow and deliver customer value efficiently.

Table 13.1   Lean and AI.

Lean Focus Area	AI Contribution	Eliminated Waste
Predictive quality control	Early defect prediction	Defects, rework
Real-time inspection	Automated defect detection	Overprocessing, labor
Demand forecasting	Aligning production with demand	Overproduction, excess inventory
Process optimization	Identifying inefficiencies and bottlenecks	Waiting, unnecessary motion
Root cause analysis	Accelerated problem identification	Defects, over-processing
Real-time monitoring	IoT integration for live process control	Delays, defects
Intelligent scheduling	Optimizing resource allocation	Downtime, underutilization
Supply chain optimization	Predicting supplier risks	Defective inputs, waiting
Task automation	Automating non-value-added tasks	Labor, motion, overprocessing

Table 13.2 shows a step-by-step guide to creating a VSM, along with ways AI can enhance each stage. To create a value stream map:

Step 1. Identify the product or service family.

- Purpose: Define the scope of the VSM, focusing on a specific product, service, or process flow that delivers value to the customer.

- Actions:
  - Identify the product or service family
  - Determine the starting and ending points of the value stream (for example, order receipt to product delivery).

Table 13.2   Value stream mapping and lean.

Steps	Description	AI Integration
1. Identify scope	Define product family and value stream.	AI analyzes historical data for key products.
2. Map current state	Document current processes, timelines, and flows.	AI automates data collection and process mining.
3. Analyze current state	Identify value-added and non-value-added steps.	AI detects waste, bottlenecks, and inefficiencies.
4. Design future state	Create optimized process flow.	AI uses simulations, predictive insights, and automation.
5. Implement improvements	Deploy changes and monitor progress.	AI tracks metrics, automates reporting, and adjusts processes.
6. Continuous improvement	Monitor and refine processes iteratively.	AI supports real-time monitoring and proactive suggestions.

AI integration:

- AI tools analyze historical data to determine which product or process has the most significant impact on costs, cycle time, or defects.

- AI-powered systems group similar processes or products to ensure accurate scoping.

Step 2. Map the current state. The current state map visualizes how things currently work within the process. Follow these steps to map the current state:

1. Gather data: Collect key metrics such as cycle time, lead time, process time, inventory levels, and defect rates for each step.

2. Document the process flow.

- Start with the customer demand and work backward.

- Draw process blocks for each step in the flow (such as manufacturing, assembly, or inspection).

3. Capture material and information flow: Identify material movement (for example, raw material to production) and information flow (such as orders or approvals).

4. Record timelines and metrics. Add data boxes for each step showing:

- Cycle time (CT): The time taken for one unit to pass through a process step.

- Lead time (LT): Total time from the start to the end of the step, including waiting times.

- Inventory or queue sizes at each step.

AI integration:

- Automated data collection: AI integrates with IoT devices, ERP systems, and sensors to automatically collect real-time data for process metrics, such as cycle times, lead times, and inventory levels.

- Process mining: AI tools analyze system logs and workflows to map the actual process flow rather than relying on assumptions or manual input.

- Bottleneck detection: ML algorithms identify bottlenecks by analyzing delays, high inventory, or resource underutilization.

- Example: AI tools highlight that a machine spends 25% of its cycle time idle, prompting further investigation.

Step 3. Analyze the current state map.

- Purpose: Identify value-added (VA) and non-value-added (NVA) activities to uncover opportunities for improvement.

- Steps:
  - Categorize each process step:
    - VA activities transform the product and are essential to meet customer requirements.
    - NVA activities do not add value but consume resources (such as waiting, inspections, or rework).
  - Use lean tools, such as the 8 Wastes (TIMWOODS):
    - Transportation, Inventory, Motion, Waiting, Overproduction, Overprocessing, Defects, Skills underutilization.

AI integration:

- Anomaly detection: AI tools flag inconsistencies or inefficiencies in cycle times, resource utilization, or process outputs.[5]

- Waste identification: AI analyzes processes to identify common lean wastes like waiting times, excess inventory, or overprocessing.[6]

- Visualization: AI generates automated visualizations of data-driven insights (such as heat maps or delay points) to support analysis.[7]

Step 4. Design the future state map. The future state map outlines the optimized process flow by eliminating waste, improving efficiency, and aligning operations with customer demand.

Steps to map the future state:

- Define customer demand. Use metrics like Takt time (the available time divided by customer demand) to determine the production rate required.

- Implement flow and pull systems.
  - Focus on achieving a continuous flow of materials with minimal waiting.

- – Implement pull systems (for example, Kanban) to produce based on demand rather than forecasts.
- Reduce NVA steps. Eliminate or automate NVA activities identified in the analysis phase.
- Integrate technology. Use AI and automation for real-time monitoring, quality control, and decision-making.
- Update metrics. Optimize process metrics like cycle time, inventory levels, and defect rates.

AI integration:

- Predictive analytics: ML predicts potential issues, such as material shortages, process delays, or quality defects, to enable proactive improvements.
- Optimized scheduling: AI automates production scheduling to align with customer demand and minimize bottlenecks.
- Continuous flow design: AI tools suggest optimal layouts for equipment and processes to ensure smooth material and information flow.
- Example: AI simulates different process flows using digital twins to identify the most efficient future state design.

Step 5. Implement the future state.

- Purpose: Deploy the improvements outlined in the future state map.
- Steps:
  1. Train employees on process changes and lean principles.
  2. Implement AI-driven systems to automate tasks like real-time quality control and demand forecasting.
  3. Monitor key metrics to ensure process changes deliver expected improvements.

Step 6. Seek continuous improvement (kaizen).

- VSM is not a one-time exercise but part of an ongoing improvement cycle. AI supports continuous improvement by providing real-time feedback, monitoring key performance indicators (KPIs), and adapting processes to changes in demand or conditions.

AI integration:

- Real-time monitoring: AI integrates with IoT and sensors to monitor the process continuously, flagging deviations.

- Automated reporting: AI dashboards provide real-time VSM updates and trend analysis.

- Feedback loops: AI learns from historical process data to suggest further improvements.

EXAMPLES OF AI TOOLS FOR VSM

1. Microsoft Power Automate integrates with Microsoft Visio to map workflows. AI-driven analytics in Power Automate helps identify bottlenecks and streamline processes, while Visio provides customizable templates to create VSMs.[8]

2. Minit Process Mining leverages AI to analyze data and create detailed process maps, including VSMs automatically from event logs. It visualizes workflows and identifies inefficiencies, such as delays or overprocessing.[9]

3. IBM Process Mining uses AI to capture and analyze process data, automatically generating process maps and offering insights into waste and inefficiencies, including process simulation and optimization.[10]

4. While not purely AI-driven, Lucidchart integrates with AI-based tools like Google Workspace AI or Microsoft Power BI for data analysis, making it easier to create dynamic and data-informed VSMs.[11]

5. UiPath Process Mining provides tools to automate process discovery and generate value stream maps from raw data, offering insights for lean and Six Sigma initiatives, including identification of bottlenecks and improvement opportunities.[12]

Conclusion: Empowering Lean with AI

AI transforms traditional process optimization methodologies by providing real-time insights, predictive analytics, and dynamic adaptability. When combined with lean and Six Sigma principles, AI enables organizations to achieve unprecedented levels of efficiency and quality. In the next chapter, we will explore how AI optimizes supply chain management to ensure seamless end-to-end operations.

Chapter 14

AI-Powered Supply Chain Quality

The supply chain is a critical component of quality management, impacting everything from raw material procurement to final product delivery. AI can greatly support supply chain quality management by enabling proactive monitoring, predictive analytics, and enhanced traceability. This chapter explores what an AI-powered supply chain can look like.

MANAGING SUPPLIER QUALITY WITH AI

In the ever-evolving landscape of supply chain management, ensuring consistent supplier performance and material quality is a critical factor in maintaining operational excellence. Traditional methods of supplier assessment and quality control, while effective in their time, often fall short in addressing the complexities and speed required in modern manufacturing and logistics. This is where advanced technologies, particularly AI, are transforming the game.

AI-powered systems provide a more dynamic, data-driven approach to managing supplier relationships and quality assurance. By leveraging historical performance data, real-time monitoring tools, and predictive analytics, organizations can proactively identify risks, streamline processes, and foster better collaboration with their suppliers. From pinpointing recurring issues to forecasting potential disruptions, these innovations enable manufacturers to uphold high-quality standards while maintaining agility in their supply chains. AI can help with:

1. Automated supplier assessment
   - AI evaluates supplier performance based on historical data, including delivery timelines, defect rates, and compliance records.

- Example: AI identifies a supplier with a recurring issue of delivering substandard materials, prompting a review and corrective action plan.[1]

2. Real-time quality monitoring

- IoT devices and AI tools monitor incoming materials for defects or inconsistencies.

- Example: Sensors detect irregularities in raw materials like moisture content in grains or impurities in metals during delivery.[2]

3. Predictive quality metrics

- ML models predict supplier performance trends, enabling proactive quality management.

- Example: AI forecasts potential delays or quality issues with a supplier based on past performance and market trends.[3]

4. Enhancing collaboration

- AI-powered platforms facilitate better communication and transparency between manufacturers and suppliers.

- Example: A shared dashboard allows suppliers to view quality expectations and real-time feedback on their deliveries.[4]

PREDICTIVE ANALYTICS FOR SUPPLY CHAIN DISRUPTIONS

In today's globalized and highly interconnected markets, supply chains face unprecedented challenges stemming from demand fluctuations, geopolitical uncertainties, and natural disasters. Traditional supply chain management strategies, often reactive and siloed, struggle to provide the agility and foresight required to maintain efficiency and resilience. This is where predictive analytics emerges as a transformative solution, enabling organizations to shift from reactive problem-solving to proactive decision-making.

Predictive analytics leverages advanced data modeling and ML techniques to anticipate potential disruptions, optimize resource allocation, and streamline operations. By analyzing historical and real-time data, it provides actionable insights into future scenarios, empowering supply chain managers to mitigate risks, enhance logistics, and improve overall efficiency. From predicting demand spikes to assessing supplier vulnerabilities, predictive analytics turns vast amounts of data into a competitive advantage. Advantages include:

1. Risk identification

   - AI analyzes external factors such as weather conditions, geopolitical events, and market volatility to predict potential supply chain risks.
   - Example: Predicting a delay in material delivery due to a hurricane affecting a key supplier's operations.

2. Demand forecasting

   - AI models anticipate demand fluctuations, enabling better inventory and production planning.
   - Example: Predicting seasonal spikes in demand for specific products and ensuring adequate stock of raw materials.

3. Logistics optimization

   - AI optimizes logistics routes and schedules to minimize delays and costs.
   - Example: Re-routing shipments to avoid congested ports or areas impacted by natural disasters.

4. Supplier risk scoring

   - AI assigns risk scores to suppliers based on various parameters, including financial stability, compliance history, and geographic risks.
   - Example: Highlighting high-risk suppliers to prioritize alternative sourcing strategies.

ENHANCING TRACEABILITY AND RECALL READINESS

Traceability is crucial for ensuring product safety and quality. AI enhances traceability by providing end-to-end visibility across the supply chain and streamlining recall processes via:

1. Blockchain integration

   - AI integrates with blockchain technology to create tamper-proof records of material and product movements.

   - Example: Tracking a batch of pharmaceuticals from raw material sourcing to final delivery, ensuring compliance with regulatory standards.[5]

2. Real-time tracking

   - IoT devices and AI monitor the location and condition of goods throughout the supply chain.

   - Example: Tracking temperature-sensitive vaccines to ensure they remain within required storage conditions during transit.[6]

3. Recall simulation

   - AI simulates recall scenarios to test readiness and identify gaps in processes.

   - Example: Running a simulated recall of contaminated food products to evaluate response times and traceability efficiency.[7]

4. Root cause identification

   - AI analyzes data to pinpoint the source of quality issues, expediting recalls and corrective actions.

   - Example: Identifying a specific supplier batch responsible for defects in a consumer product line.[8]

CASE STUDY: AI-DRIVEN SUPPLY CHAIN RESILIENCE IN ELECTRONICS MANUFACTURING

Scenario: An electronics manufacturer faced frequent disruptions due to unreliable suppliers and global shipping delays.

Solutions:

1. Supplier quality management

   - AI assessed supplier performance data, highlighting vendors with consistent quality issues.

   - Recommendations included transitioning to alternate suppliers with better performance metrics.

2. Predictive analytics

   - ML models forecasted potential disruptions from geopolitical tensions and material shortages.

   - AI optimized production schedules based on predicted delays, ensuring minimal downtime.

3. Enhanced traceability

   - AI integrated with blockchain to provide end-to-end visibility of raw materials and components.

   - IoT devices tracked shipments, ensuring on-time delivery and compliance with handling requirements.

The company used SAP Ariba[9] to assess supplier performance data, identifying vendors with recurring quality issues. The AI system recommended transitioning to alternate suppliers with better performance and reliability metrics. ML models powered by IBM Planning Analytics with Watson[10] forecasted disruptions due to geopolitical tensions and material shortages. Based on these predictions, AI optimized production schedules, reducing downtime and ensuring efficient resource allocation. The manufacturer deployed Oracle Blockchain Platform[11] to integrate AI and blockchain for end-to-end visibility of raw materials and components. IoT devices, managed via AWS IoT Core,[12] tracked shipments in real-time, ensuring on-time delivery and compliance with handling requirements.

Outcomes:

- Supply chain disruptions reduced by 30% within the first year.
- On-time production rates improved by 20%.
- Recall readiness was enhanced, reducing response time for defective products by 40%.

Conclusion: Transforming Supply Chain Quality with AI

AI empowers organizations to manage supplier quality, predict disruptions, and enhance traceability with unprecedented precision and efficiency. By adopting AI-driven tools, businesses can build resilient supply chains, ensure consistent product quality, and maintain customer trust. The next chapter will focus on the ethical implications of AI in quality management and strategies for building trust in AI systems.

Chapter 15
Risk Management with AI

In modern times, any quality management program is incomplete without a risk management component. Risk management has proven to be a cornerstone of operational excellence. AI provides innovative tools to enhance traditional risk management practices by automating the creation of failure mode and effects analysis (FMEA), hazard analysis, suggesting risk controls, and enabling real-time risk monitoring. This chapter first assesses the risk of AI itself and then explores how AI revolutionizes risk management.

RISK MANAGEMENT AND AI LIFE CYCLE

The AI life cycle is described in ISO/IEC 22989:2022[1] (discussed in Chapter 19). We will take a look at risk management deliverables in each life cycle phase, but before we do that let us discuss top-level organization requirements for risk management per guidance in ISO/IEC 23894:2023[2]:

1. The top management should commit resources for AI risk management and establish general criteria for acceptability of these risks and a framework for assessing these risks.

2. The documentation requirements or the deliverables of the risk management process as it relates to assessment of AI should be clear and embedded in the workflow of the organization's risk management framework.

3. The risk management framework should address:

   - Risk acceptability criteria in the form of risk matrices etc.

   - Potential risk sources

   - Techniques for risk assessment

- Techniques for monitoring and controlling risk
- Risk reporting

LIFE CYCLE PHASE 1: INCEPTION

The inception phase is the feasibility or the concept phase of the AI system. At this point, the organization should already have established risk management criteria and a framework that can be used to identify general risks related to AI. A good place to start risk identification is by reviewing the organizational objectives in relation to the AI. The goal here is to prioritize the components and interfaces of the AI so top-level risk controls can be generated. This exercise can lead to an overall AI system risk level and can also lead to the discovery of new requirements to reduce the risk of AI to acceptable level. ISO/IEC 42001:2023 describes several potential AI-related organizational objectives and risk sources. These objectives pertain to accountability, expertise, availability and quality of training and test data, environmental impact, fairness, maintainability, privacy, robustness, safety, security, transparency, and explainability.

PHASE 2: DESIGN AND DEVELOPMENT

The design and development process starts with defining user needs and the associated design requirements of the AI system. The initial risk assessment in the previous phase, which was more generic, is now refined to include scenarios where the requirement is not met or the output deviates from the expected. This means the continuous update of the initial risk assessment in more technical detail. Newer risk controls will be brainstormed in this phase, which will act as new requirements and make the AI system safer and more effective. The risk controls should always be verified and validated. ISO/IEC 42001:2023 describes several potential AI-related risk sources such as complexity of environment, lack of transparency and explain ability, level of automation, ML and quality of data used for it, system hardware issues, system life-cycle issues such as flaws and design, inadequate deployment, lack of maintenance, and technological readiness.

PHASE 3: VERIFICATION AND VALIDATION

During verification and validation testing, the risk control or treatment plans for the system, its interfaces, or its components is created, assessed, and adjusted. The risk controls that were decided in the previous phase should undergo verification. If a particular control fails verification or validation, then a better control should be put in place. In this stage, the verification of implementation and verification of effectiveness of the risk control are reported.

PHASE 4: DEPLOYMENT

The deployment phase is when the AI system as a whole is up and running either in a beta or real-world environment. This serves as a real-world validation and might lead to configuration changes. The risk assessments should be continuously performed, and where any tweaks or changes to the system lead to changes in requirements, the risks should be reassessed and risk controls should be adjusted.

PHASE 5: OPERATION AND MONITORING

In the operations phase, the AI is expected to give outputs based on its design. However, this may not always be the case; therefore, we need continuous monitoring and feedback to improve AI output. These feedback reports might lead to changes in AI parameters and newer risks. This means the designers and architects still need to carry out risk reassessments every time critical feedback is received and apply appropriate risk controls to ensure the AI outputs meet the design intent.

PHASE 6: CONTINUOUS VALIDATION AND RE-EVALUATION

As the AI is live and working in real-world scenarios, it requires frequent fine-tuning, updates, and patches. This necessitates the need for continuous validation against the previously assessed objective and requirements of the system. The feedback received through the monitoring channels might prompt re-evaluation and re-examination of the system objectives in relation to the previously decided objectives of the organization and its stakeholders. All of this requires a reassessment of the risk associated with any of the changes. The goal of reassessment is to apply risk controls to ensure the output of the AI system is in alignment with what the organization intends.

PHASE 7: RETIREMENT

The top management of the organization will have to make a decision as to when the AI system will be retired. In terms of risk management there are two items that need to be addressed in this phase. First, the risk of data, information, and the model itself should be addressed. The destruction, degaussing, or removal of data by other means should be confirmed in this phase. Second, if the AI system is being replaced by another system, then this phase triggers a new risk management process with new objectives, new requirements, and new design inputs. This will require the generation of a new risk assessment and application of new risk controls.

Table 15.1 shows an example of a sample AI risk assessment that starts at the inception phase and gets more granular and detailed as it goes through the life-cycle phases.

Now let us see how AI itself can help in quality risk management activities in the latter half of the chapter.

ENTERPRISE RISK AND RISK REGISTER

A risk register is a critical tool for managing enterprise-wide risks. AI enhances the creation, maintenance, and use of risk registers, enabling organizations to identify, assess, and monitor risks with greater precision and efficiency.

A major benefit is that AI removes the manual and administrative tasks of initial population of risks and risk register, thereby allowing quality professionals to focus on discussing and treating these risks. A risk register can help with:

Table 15.1 Sample AI risk assessment (risk register).

Risk ID	AI Risk Category	AI Risk	Potential Impact	Likeli-hood (L)	Severity (S)	Risk Score (L × S)	Risk Control	Residual Risk	Verification of Risk Controls
AI-001	Bias & Fairness	Algorithmic bias	Discriminatory outcomes affecting marginalized groups	4	5	20 (High)	Regular bias audits, diverse training data, fairness-aware algorithms	Medium	Bias testing reports, fairness dashboard, external audits
AI-002	Explain-ability	Lack of model transparency	Users unable to trust or challenge AI decisions	3	4	12 (Medium)	Use of explainable AI (XAI) techniques, model documentation	Low	XAI reports, user feedback evaluation, explainability metrics
AI-003	Security	Adversarial attacks	AI manipulated to produce incorrect outputs	5	5	25 (High)	Robust adversarial testing, model hardening, anomaly detection	Medium	Penetration testing, red teaming, adversarial robustness benchmarks
AI-004	Data Privacy	Unauthorized data access	Exposure of personal/sensitive data	4	5	20 (High)	Data encryption, strict access control, federated learning	Low	Privacy impact assessments (PIA), security audits, compliance checks
AI-005	Perform-ance	Model drift	Reduced accuracy due to evolving data trends	4	4	16 (High)	Continuous monitoring, retraining on updated data	Medium	Model performance tracking, A/B testing, periodic validation

continued

Table 15.1 Sample AI risk assessment (risk register) – *continued.*

Risk ID	AI Risk Category	AI Risk	Potential Impact	Likeli-hood (L)	Severity (S)	Risk Score (L × S)	Risk Control	Residual Risk	Verification of Risk Controls
AI-006	Ethical Compliance	Unintended conse-quences	AI generates harmful or unethical outputs	3	5	15 (High)	AI ethics review, reinforcement learning with human feedback (RLHF)	Medium	AI ethics committee reviews, simulated scenario testing
AI-007	Regulatory Compliance	Non-compliance with laws	Fines, legal penalties, reputation damage	3	5	15 (High)	Regular legal audits, adherence to GDPR/AI Act/ISO 42001	Low	Compliance audits, legal assessments, certification attainment
AI-008	System Reliability	Model failure or downtime	Service disruption impacting critical functions	3	5	15 (High)	Redundancy planning, failover systems, robustness testing	Low	Incident reports, uptime monitoring, failover system tests
AI-009	User Safety	Unsafe automation	AI system makes harmful real-world decisions	2	5	10 (Medium)	Human-in-the-loop validation, simulation-based safety tests	Low	Safety validation reports, real-world testing, oversight logs
AI-010	Misinfor-mation	Hallucination	AI generates false or misleading content	4	4	16 (High)	Fact-checking mechanisms, retrieval-augmented generation (RAG)	Medium	Misinformation detection rates, accuracy benchmarking

1. AI-driven risk identification

    *   AI scans organizational data, including operational logs, financial records, and compliance reports, to identify potential risks.

    *   Example: A multinational corporation uses IBM OpenPages[3] to scan operational logs, procurement data, and supplier payments. The AI system identifies emerging risks, such as delayed supplier payments linked to potential financial instability, enabling proactive mitigation.

2. Automated risk scoring

    *   AI evaluates the severity, likelihood, and impact of risks, assigning them scores to prioritize mitigation efforts.

    *   Example: Assigning a high-risk score to geopolitical risks affecting key suppliers based on market data.

3. Dynamic updates

    *   AI continuously updates the risk register as new data become available, ensuring it remains relevant and actionable.

    *   Example: Use of Data Reality's[4] Intellirisk ML model to create a cybersecurity risk assessment that automatically populates based on CVE database updates using CVSS scoring for risk.

4. Enhanced reporting and visualization

    *   AI-powered dashboards provide real-time views of the risk landscape, highlighting critical areas for immediate attention.

    *   Example: A heat map visualization showing high-risk areas across global operations.

5. Integration with risk controls

    *   The risk register integrates seamlessly with AI-driven risk controls to monitor mitigation effectiveness.

- Example: Linking a high-risk item to automated controls that enforce compliance with safety protocols.

Benefits include centralized risk management for improved oversight; enhanced collaboration across departments through shared, up-to-date risk data; and proactive identification and mitigation of enterprise risks.

CYBERSECURITY RISK MANAGEMENT

AI plays a pivotal role in managing cybersecurity risks by detecting threats, predicting vulnerabilities, and automating incident responses. Organizations can leverage AI to safeguard sensitive data, ensure system integrity, and comply with regulatory requirements. Consider:

1. Threat detection and prevention

   - AI identifies potential cybersecurity threats by analyzing network traffic, user behavior, and system logs.

   - Example: AI can detect unusual login patterns that indicate a potential phishing attack. CrowdStrike Falcon[5] uses AI to analyze network traffic, system logs, and user behavior, detecting unusual login patterns that may indicate phishing or other cyberattacks.

2. Predictive vulnerability analysis

   - ML models predict vulnerabilities in systems based on historical breach data and current configurations.

   - Example: AI can highlight outdated software versions that are susceptible to known exploits. Tenable.io[6] leverages ML to predict system vulnerabilities by analyzing historical breach data and current configurations. It highlights risks such as outdated software versions vulnerable to known exploits.

3. Automated incident response

   - AI systems automate responses to cybersecurity incidents, reducing reaction times.

- Example: You can automatically isolate a compromised device from the network to prevent further breaches. Cortex XSOAR[7] automates incident response processes by isolating compromised devices and executing pre-defined response playbooks, minimizing the spread of breaches.

4. Continuous monitoring

- AI continuously monitors systems for suspicious activities, ensuring real-time protection.

- Example: AI can flag a sudden increase in data transfers that may indicate a data exfiltration attempt. Darktrace[8] uses AI to continuously monitor systems for anomalies, flagging suspicious activities such as a sudden increase in data transfers that may indicate a data exfiltration attempt.

AI IN FMEA AND HAZARD ANALYSIS

Using FMEA and hazard analysis are systematic approaches for identifying and mitigating potential failures and risks. AI enhances these processes by automating the creation, updating, and prioritization of risks, making them more efficient and effective. You can use:

1. AI-assisted FMEA creation

- AI analyzes historical data, maintenance logs, and production records to identify potential failure modes.

- Example: An AI tool scans machine performance data to automatically populate an FMEA with high-risk components and their associated failure modes. AI models such as Data Reality's Intellirisk[9] can automatically populate any FMEA or hazard analysis template.

2. Dynamic risk prioritization

- AI assigns and updates risk levels, action priorities, and risk priority numbers (RPNs) based on real-time data inputs. These can be later verified and discussed with the risk team.

- Example: AI recalculates RPNs when a machine's wear rate increases, prioritizing it for preventive maintenance.

3. Automated hazard identification

   - AI detects hazards by analyzing operational data, complaints, post market data, environmental conditions, and compliance records.

   - Example: AI identifies that temperature fluctuations in a storage unit increase the risk of product degradation.

4. Integrated root cause analysis

   - AI correlates failure data with operational conditions to pinpoint root causes.

   - Example: AI links frequent bearing failures to misaligned shafts detected through sensor data.

AI-DRIVEN RISK CONTROLS

Risk controls aim to mitigate or eliminate identified risks. AI suggests actionable and data-driven risk controls tailored to specific scenarios. You may utilize:

1. Proactive recommendations

   - AI recommends control measures based on historical data and predictive analytics.

   - Example: Suggesting changes to operating procedures to reduce the likelihood of human error during a critical process.

2. Adaptive control implementation

   - AI dynamically adjusts controls based on real-time monitoring.

   - Example: Increasing ventilation in a factory when sensors detect high levels of volatile organic compounds.

3. Regulatory compliance

- AI ensures that risk controls align with regulatory requirements.
- Example: Flagging a chemical handling process that does not meet OSHA standards and recommending corrective actions.

4. Continuous improvement

- AI learns from past incidents to refine risk controls and improve effectiveness.
- Example: Modifying safety protocols based on trends in incident reports.

REAL-TIME RISK MONITORING AND MITIGATION

AI enables organizations to monitor risks continuously, detect anomalies, and respond in real time to mitigate potential issues.

1. IoT-driven monitoring

- Sensors capture operational data, and AI analyzes them to identify potential risks.
- Example: Detecting vibrations in machinery that indicate impending failure and triggering an alert.

2. Early warning systems

- ML models predict risks before they escalate.
- Example: Predicting supply chain disruptions due to geopolitical events and enabling proactive sourcing.

3. Risk dashboards

- AI-powered dashboards provide real-time visualizations of risk metrics across operations.
- Example: Displaying a heat map of high-risk areas in a production facility for quick decision-making.

4. Automated mitigation actions

- AI executes predefined mitigation protocols when risks exceed thresholds.

- Example: Shutting down a reactor automatically when pressure levels rise dangerously high.

CASE STUDY: AI-POWERED FMEA IN PHARMACEUTICALS

Scenario: A pharmaceutical manufacturer needed to identify and mitigate the risks associated with temperature-sensitive raw materials.

Solution:

1. Automated hazard analysis

- AI analyzed historical storage data and identified fluctuations in temperature as a critical hazard.

- The FMEA sheet was automatically populated with risks related to temperature excursions and their potential impacts on product quality.

2. Dynamic risk controls

- AI recommended installing advanced cooling systems and implementing real-time temperature monitoring as risk controls based on risk prioritization in FMEA.

- It also suggested contingency plans, such as relocating materials to alternative storage facilities during equipment downtime.

3. Real-time monitoring

- IoT sensors monitored storage conditions, and AI provided alerts for deviations.

- Automated adjustments to cooling systems ensured materials remained within safe temperature ranges.

Outcomes:

- Material loss was reduced due to temperature excursions by 50%.

- Compliance with regulatory standards for temperature-sensitive materials improved.

- Operational efficiency increased as a result of integrating AI-driven hazard analysis with quality management systems.

Conclusion: AI as a Catalyst for Proactive Risk Management

By automating FMEA creation, suggesting effective risk controls, and enabling real-time risk monitoring, AI transforms risk management from a reactive process into a proactive strategy. Organizations can achieve greater efficiency, compliance, and resilience, ensuring operational excellence in an increasingly complex environment.

Chapter 16
Training and Knowledge Management in the AI Era

The rapid integration of AI in quality assurance and quality control (QA/QC) demands a parallel evolution in training and knowledge management. AI-driven tools offer new ways to train employees, maintain institutional knowledge, and provide on-demand expertise. This chapter explores how AI can support employee training, knowledge repositories, and expert systems.

AI TOOLS FOR EMPLOYEE TRAINING AND CERTIFICATION

AI enhances employee training by personalizing learning experiences, automating assessments, and ensuring continuous skill development. Some examples are listed here:

1. Personalized learning paths

   - AI adapts training programs to individual employee needs based on their role, performance, and learning preferences.

   - Example: An AI system designs a custom training module for a QA inspector focusing on advanced statistical techniques.

2. Real-time skill assessments

   - AI evaluates employees through simulations and quizzes, identifying areas for improvement.

   - Example: A virtual reality-based training tool assesses an operator's proficiency in performing complex equipment setups. STRIVR[1] uses virtual reality (VR) to simulate real-world scenarios and assess employee skills. For example, operators can be evaluated on their proficiency in setting up complex machinery through immersive VR training.

3. Automated certification management

   - AI tracks employee certifications, schedules renewals, and recommends courses to maintain compliance.

   - Example: Cornerstone[2] uses AI to track employee certifications, automatically schedule renewals, and recommend courses for maintaining compliance. For instance, a lab technician receives alerts to renew their ISO 13485 certification and access to approved training programs.

4. Gamification and engagement

   - AI introduces gamified elements like leaderboards, rewards, and challenges to make learning engaging.

   - Example: Kahoot![3] incorporates gamified learning through leaderboards, rewards, and challenges, making training engaging. Employees earn badges for completing AI-driven training modules on quality audits.

CREATING A KNOWLEDGE REPOSITORY WITH AI

AI transforms traditional knowledge management systems into dynamic, searchable, and continuously updated repositories. It may be used for:

1. Automated data organization

   - AI categorizes and indexes documents, training materials, and best practices for easy access.

   - Example: M-Files[4] uses AI to categorize and index documents, training materials, and best practices automatically. For example, quality manuals and SOPs are tagged with relevant keywords based on their content, making them easier to locate.

2. A searchable knowledge base

- NLP enables employees to retrieve relevant information using conversational queries.
- Example: Bloomfire[5] leverages NLP to enable employees to retrieve relevant information using conversational queries. For example, typing "How to calibrate the XYZ machine?" returns a detailed step-by-step guide instantly.

3. Knowledge retention

- AI captures institutional knowledge from retiring employees through interviews and document analysis.
- Example: Syntheia[6] captures institutional knowledge from retiring employees through interviews and document analysis. For instance, it records a senior engineer's troubleshooting techniques and integrates them into a searchable database for future reference.

4. Continuous updates

- AI integrates with operational systems to keep the repository updated with the latest standards and practices.
- Example: Confluence[7] integrates with operational systems to keep knowledge repositories updated. For example, it automatically updates SOPs when new regulatory requirements are introduced, ensuring compliance.

Conclusion: Building a Smarter Workforce

AI revolutionizes training and knowledge management by personalizing learning, preserving expertise, and providing on-demand support. By leveraging these tools, organizations can empower their workforce, ensure seamless knowledge transfer, and drive continuous improvement in quality management practices. In the next chapter, we will explore the ethical implications of AI in quality management and strategies for building trust in AI-driven systems.

Chapter 17

Ethical Considerations and Challenges

The adoption of AI in quality brings transformative benefits, but it also raises ethical considerations. Organizations must navigate challenges such as data privacy, model bias, and maintaining human oversight to build trust in AI systems. This chapter explores these key challenges and provides strategies for ethical AI deployment.

DATA PRIVACY AND SECURITY

AI systems often require access to vast amounts of data, raising concerns about privacy and security. Ensuring data integrity and compliance with regulations is critical to maintaining stakeholder trust. When using AI, you must consider the importance of:

1. Ensuring data privacy

   - Use anonymization techniques to remove personally identifiable information (PII) from datasets.
   - Example: Anonymize customer complaint data before analyzing it for quality trends.

2. Compliance with regulations

   - Align AI practices with data protection laws such as GDPR, HIPAA, or CCPA.
   - Example: Implement stringent access controls to comply with HIPAA when handling medical device data.

3. Data security measures

   - Employ robust encryption, firewalls, and intrusion detection systems to protect data.

- Example: Encrypt supply chain data to prevent unauthorized access during analysis.

4. Regular audits

- Conduct periodic security audits of AI systems to identify vulnerabilities.

- Example: Evaluate an AI-driven SPC system to ensure compliance with ISO 27001 standards.

BIAS IN AI/ML MODELS: IDENTIFICATION AND MITIGATION

AI models can unintentionally amplify biases present in training data, leading to unfair or inaccurate outcomes. Proactively identifying and mitigating bias is essential for ethical AI deployment. Ensure that you are:

1. Identifying bias

- Use fairness metrics to assess model outputs for disparities across different groups.

- Example: Evaluate an AI system for defect detection to ensure it doesn't disproportionately flag products from specific suppliers.

2. Using diverse training data

- Ensure datasets are representative of all relevant scenarios and populations.

- Example: Include diverse environmental conditions in training data for a predictive maintenance model.

3. Using explainable tools

- Leverage tools like SHAP (SHapley Additive exPlanations) to understand model decision-making processes.

- Example: Use SHAP to explain why an AI system flagged certain batches for quality review.

4. Completing regular model reviews

- Continuously evaluate AI models for performance and fairness as new data become available.
- Example: Updating a demand forecasting model to address biases caused by historical seasonality.

BALANCING AUTOMATION WITH HUMAN OVERSIGHT

While automation improves efficiency, human oversight remains essential for ensuring ethical decision-making and addressing complex scenarios beyond AI's scope. Be sure to:

1. Use human-in-the-loop (HITL) systems

- Integrate human review into AI workflows for critical decisions.
- Example: Require QA managers to approve AI-generated non-conformance reports before implementation.

2. Establish accountability

- Define clear roles and responsibilities for AI oversight.
- Example: Assign a dedicated team to monitor and validate AI-driven risk assessments.

3. Train for ethical AI use

- Educate employees on the limitations of AI and the importance of ethical considerations.
- Example: Conduct workshops on recognizing and addressing AI biases in quality control.

4. Use escalation protocols

- Design AI systems to escalate ambiguous or high-risk scenarios to human experts.
- Example: Flag outlier data during a production run for manual review before halting operations.

CASE STUDY: ENSURING ETHICAL AI IN MEDICAL DEVICE MANUFACTURING

Scenario: A medical device manufacturer implemented an AI-powered system but faced challenges with data privacy and model fairness.

Solution:

1. Data privacy measures

   - The manufacturer deployed anonymization techniques to protect patient data used for training the AI system.

   - They implemented encryption and multi-factor authentication for data access.

2. Bias mitigation

   - The manufacturer conducted fairness audits to ensure the system's defect detection rates were consistent across different device models.

   - The model was retrained using diverse datasets to improve fairness.

3. Human oversight

   - An HITL review process was established for flagged defects.

   - Trained QA teams interpreted AI insights and identified potential biases.

Outcomes:

   - Trust in the AI system improved among stakeholders.

   - The manufacturer achieved compliance with GDPR and ISO 13485 standards.

   - Defect detection errors were reduced by 20% while maintaining ethical practices.

Conclusion: Building Trust in AI

Ethical AI deployment is essential for maintaining stakeholder confidence and achieving sustainable quality management. By addressing data privacy, mitigating bias, and balancing automation with human oversight, organizations can harness AI's potential while upholding ethical standards. In the next chapter, we will explore the future of AI in quality management and its potential to shape the next generation of QA/QC practices.

Chapter 18
AI and Reliability

Reliability is a critical and foundational part of quality management, ensuring that products and systems perform consistently under specified conditions. AI has large capability to enhance reliability management by enabling predictive maintenance and failure analysis, and inculcating robust design processes. This chapter explores how AI tools and techniques impact and can transform the field of reliability engineering.

AI APPLICATIONS IN RELIABILITY MANAGEMENT

You may use the following AI applications for management:

1. Predictive maintenance

   - AI models can help analyze equipment data to forecast potential failures and recommend maintenance before issues arise.

   - Example: Use sensor data to predict bearing wear in machinery, reducing unplanned downtime.

2. Fault detection and diagnostics

   - AI model can detect faults and anomalies in systems by analyzing real-time and historical data to trigger alerts.

   - Techniques:

     - Anomaly detection uses unsupervised ML algorithms (for example, Isolation Forests, Autoencoders) to detect abnormal behavior.[1]

     - Pattern recognition recognizes failure signatures or patterns.

     - Sensor fusion integrates multiple sensors (for example, IoT) to identify faults accurately.

3. Failure analysis

   - ML can identify patterns in failure data to uncover root causes and inform corrective actions.

   - Example: TIBCO Spotfire[2] analyzes historical failure data to uncover patterns and root causes, such as identifying a specific supplier's material linked to recurring product defects. A manufacturer uses Spotfire to analyze defect data and finds that material from one supplier contributes disproportionately to failure rates, prompting a supplier review.

4. Reliability testing optimization

   - AI can optimize reliability testing by simulating various scenarios and stress conditions.

   - Example: Running virtual tests on a new electronic device design to predict its lifespan under different environmental conditions.[3] ANSYS uses AI and simulation to test product designs under virtual stress conditions. It predicts lifespans and failure points for electronic devices by simulating various environmental scenarios.

5. Warranty and life-cycle predictions

   - AI model can forecast product life cycles and warranty claims based on usage patterns and failure data.

   - Example: AI can predict warranty claim trends for automotive components to inform design improvements.[4]

AI applications in the field of reliability are summarized in Table 18.1.

ENHANCING RELIABILITY DESIGN WITH AI

1. Robust design

   - AI enhances the robustness of products by identifying design parameters that reduce variability and improve performance.

Table 18.1 AI and reliability impact.

Area	AI Contribution	Benefit
Predictive maintenance	Forecasts failures and optimizes maintenance	Reduces downtime and over-maintenance
Fault detection	Identifies anomalies and triggers alerts	Early fault identification
Root cause analysis	Pinpoints failure causes using data analysis	Faster problem-solving
Reliability prediction	Estimates remaining useful life (RUL)	Proactive replacements
Reliability testing	Simulates failures with digital twins	Reduces physical testing costs
Real-time monitoring	Integrates IoT for live system monitoring	Immediate intervention
FMEA automation	Automates failure mode identification	Improves risk prioritization
Continuous improvement	Feeds failure data into ongoing model updates	Enhances long-term reliability

- Example: ANSYS Fluent[5] uses AI-powered simulations to optimize designs for robustness, such as identifying parameters that allow turbine blades to withstand extreme temperatures and reduce variability in performance.

2. Design of experiments (DOE):

- AI accelerates DOE by analyzing complex interactions between variables and recommending optimal designs.

- Example: Minitab Engage[6] leverages AI to accelerate DOE by analyzing interactions between variables and suggesting optimal design configurations. For example, it helps identify the best combination of materials and coatings for corrosion-resistant components.

3. Failure mode avoidance

   - AI integrates with CAD tools to simulate failure scenarios and recommend design adjustments.

   - Example: Autodesk Fusion 360[7] integrates AI with CAD tools to simulate failure scenarios and recommend design adjustments. For example, AI identifies stress points in a bridge design and recommends reinforcements to avoid structural failure.

4. Digital twins

   - AI-powered digital models simulate real-world conditions to predict system behavior.

   - Example: Siemens Simcenter[8] creates AI-powered digital twins to simulate real-world conditions and predict system behavior.

REAL-TIME RELIABILITY MONITORING

To ensure AI is performing correctly, monitor reliability via:

1. IoT and AI integration

   - Various IoT devices provide real-time data on system performance, which AI analyzes to detect anomalies.

   - Example: AWS IoT Analytics[9] integrates IoT devices with AI to monitor real-time data and detect anomalies. For example, it tracks temperature fluctuations in a refrigeration system to ensure consistent cooling and prevent spoilage.

2. Early warning systems

   - AI systems issue alerts for potential reliability issues before they escalate.

   - Example: IBM Watson IoT Platform[10] uses AI to analyze data from IoT sensors, issuing alerts for potential reliability issues. For instance, it flags an increase in vibration levels in a pump as an early indicator of failure.

3. Dynamic reliability models

   - AI updates reliability models in real time based on new data, ensuring they remain accurate and actionable.

   - Example: Siemens MindSphere[11] creates dynamic reliability models by analyzing real-time IoT data. For example, it adjusts reliability estimates for wind turbines based on weather patterns and operational performance data.

CASE STUDY: AI-DRIVEN RELIABILITY IN AEROSPACE

Scenario: An aerospace manufacturer faced challenges in ensuring the reliability of jet engines, which operate under extreme conditions.

Solution:

1. Predictive maintenance: AI analyzed vibration, temperature, and pressure data from engine sensors to predict component wear.

2. Failure analysis: ML identified correlations between operating conditions and failures, guiding design improvements.

3. Real-time monitoring: Various IoT devices and AI monitored engine performance during flights, issuing alerts for maintenance needs.

Outcomes:

- In-flight engine failures reduced by 20%.

- Engine life was extended by 25% through optimized maintenance schedules.

- Customer satisfaction and safety metrics improved.

Conclusion: AI as a Catalyst for Reliability Excellence

AI empowers organizations to achieve new levels of reliability by enabling predictive insights, optimizing designs, and providing real-time monitoring. By integrating AI into reliability management, businesses can enhance product performance, reduce costs, and exceed customer expectations. As AI technologies continue to evolve, their potential to revolutionize reliability engineering will only grow.

Chapter 19
The AI Life Cycle

The life cycle of an AI system encompasses all stages of its life, which include its development, deployment, maintenance, and eventual retirement. We will use the ISO/IEC 22989: 2022 standard as a benchmark that provides globally accepted and structured phases for the AI system life cycle. This chapter outlines key stages of this life cycle based on this ISO standard.

There are seven AI system life-cycle stages that are described below:

1. Inception: This phase involves defining the AI system—its objectives, scope, purpose, and feasibility. This also involves defining key design requirements for the AI system that should arise from the business and stakeholder requirements. This is the phase in which a risk assessment should be done so the risks associated with the AI and its objectives can be documented and prioritized, and appropriate controls can be identified. These can then become the new requirements for the system. Risk assessment should also focus on items such as data confidentiality, availability, integrity, and privacy so all the appropriate regulatory and compliance requirements are dealt with in a risk-based manner. See Chapter 15 for additional details on risk sources and AI risk assessment.

2. Design and development: This stage focuses on designing the AI architecture, selecting algorithms, preparing data, data training, and validation. This phase includes choosing the appropriate AI model, realizing the design solutions around data collection, data processing, and augmentation. Training of the AI model using supervised, unsupervised, or reinforcement learning will also take place in this phase as part of design and development. Design and development is

the most critical phase for application of the most effective risk control measures. The risk assessment in this phase should be continuously updated with appropriate risk control measures.

3. Verification and validation: Verification and validation ensure that the AI systems meet performance, reliability, and compliance requirements. This includes model validation using test data and evaluation metrics, ensuring AI robustness, bias mitigation and generalization, and conducting security testing with adversarial robustness assessments. Verification testing can include verification to ensure that the output of the AI system matches the input in the form of the design requirement. This also serves as verification of implementation and the effectiveness of the risk control measure related to that particular requirement. The output of this phase is in the form of test data, test reports, and sometimes a verification and validation file. Risk monitoring and review should be ongoing in this phase.

4. Deployment: In this phase, the AI system is integrated into real-world environment. This includes integration with existing IT systems, cloud, or edge computing. Due to the feedback loop being critical to the success of AI models, scalability and adaptability to changing conditions are essential for the success of AI. This can be accomplished by implementing real-time monitoring and feedback mechanisms that are verified, validated, and continuously monitored. Monitoring should also address ethical concerns and bias in real-world use scenarios.

5. Operation and monitoring: Once deployed, continuous monitoring ensures AI performance and compliance with expectations. This phase includes the routine operation of the AI under normal conditions that involve operating data input, and model execution on a routine basis. The model drift should be successfully handled through real-time retraining and optimization. Monitoring AI includes risk monitoring related to reliability, safety, compliance, and security,

including logging and tracking of AI outputs for anomalies. Every time a critical issue arises, a risk reassessment should be carried out using the same risk model or framework as used for the original assessment in earlier phases. Guided by the risk acceptability criteria, appropriate risk controls should be identified for issues, and they should be verified and validated before being pushed to the deployed model.

6. Continuous validation and re-evaluation: AI systems require ongoing validation to adapt to new data and evolving environments. This stage includes retraining AI models with updated datasets, reassessing fairness, bias, and ethical implications. This phase also involves evaluating performance drift and ensuring continued compliance and expected outputs. The goal of this phase is continuous improvement. Decision-making in the re-evaluation phase involves the evaluation of AI outputs, which are the operating results that can lead to the refinement of objectives and design requirements. This can lead to new risk assessments and new risk controls.

7. Retirement: AI systems are retired when they become obsolete, unreliable, or fail to meet performance, ethical, or regulatory standards. It is important to decommission AI components responsibly. This includes disposal of data and the model. Consideration should be given to retaining essential data for audits or compliance records. A full impact assessment should be carried out for assessing the long-term impact of AI retirement and transitioning to other AI models or alternative solutions.

Understanding the AI system life cycle ensures responsible AI development, deployment, and maintenance. By following the ISO/IEC 22989: 2022 standard, organizations can create AI systems that are efficient, ethical, transparent, and adaptable. Life-cycle management helps align AI with user expectations, industry best practices, and regulatory compliance, ensuring sustainable and impactful AI adoption.

Appendix A

List of Large Language Models (LLMs)

Here's a list of NLP LLMs available for open use by the public, categorized by their licensing and accessibility:

Open-Source LLMs

These models are free to use, modify, and deploy under open licenses.

Hugging Face Transformers

- BERT (Bidirectional Encoder Representations from Transformers):
  - Focus: Text classification, sentiment analysis, and question answering.
  - Available at: https://huggingface.co/
- GPT-Neo and GPT-J (by EleutherAI):
  - Focus: General text generation, conversational AI, and code generation.
  - Available at: https://www.eleuther.ai/artifacts/gpt-neo
- RoBERTa (A Robustly Optimized BERT Pretraining Approach):
  - Focus: Enhanced NLP tasks with improved performance over BERT.
  - Available at: https://huggingface.co/
- DistilBERT:
  - Focus: Lightweight, faster version of BERT for mobile applications.
  - Available at: https://huggingface.co/

Meta's LLaMA (Large Language Model Meta AI):

- Focus: General-purpose LLM for NLP and conversational AI.
- Requires an application for research or development access.
- Available at: LLaMA Repository

Bloom (BigScience):

- Focus: Multilingual NLP and generative tasks.
- Available at: https://huggingface.co/bigscience/bloom

Open Assistant (LAION):

- Focus: Conversational AI similar to ChatGPT.
- Available at: Open Assistant

Falcon (Technology Innovation Institute):

- Focus: General text generation and NLP tasks.
- Available at: https://huggingface.co/docs/transformers/main/en/model_doc/falcon

Freemium and Public API Access

These LLMs are free for limited use but may require subscriptions for extended access.

OpenAI Models:

- GPT-4 and GPT-3.5:
  - Focus: General-purpose conversational AI, text analysis, and creative writing.
  - Access via: OpenAI API
- Codex:
  - Focus: Programming and code generation.
  - Available at: OpenAI Codex

Google's LaMDA (Language Model for Dialogue Applications):

- Focus: Conversational applications and virtual assistants.
- Available via: Google AI

Anthropic's Claude:

- Focus: Safe and conversational generative AI tasks.
- Available at: Anthropic

  AI21 Labs' Jurassic-2:

- Focus: Text generation and understanding with a large vocabulary.
- Available at: https://www.ai21.com/

Cohere Command:

- Focus: Text understanding, summarization, and classification.
- Available at: Cohere

Hosted Platforms Offering LLMs

These platforms provide LLMs via APIs or hosted services.

Hugging Face Inference API:

- Offers hosted versions of open-source models like GPT-Neo, Bloom, and Falcon.
- Available at: https://huggingface.co/docs/huggingface_hub/ en/package_reference/inference_client

Azure OpenAI Service:

- Provides hosted access to OpenAI's GPT models.
- Available at: Azure OpenAI

Google Vertex AI:

- Hosts LaMDA and other proprietary models for NLP tasks.
- Available at: https://cloud.google.com/vertex-ai

IBM Watson NLP:

- Focus: Business applications like customer support, insights extraction, and chatbot development.
- Available at: https://www.ibm.com/account/reg/us-en/signup?formid=urx-52753

Research Access LLMs

These models are often released for academic or research purposes.

T5 (Text-to-Text Transfer Transformer):

- Focus: Text generation and comprehension tasks.
- Available at: https://huggingface.co/docs/transformers/en/model_doc/t5GPT-2 (by OpenAI):
- Focus: Text generation with fewer restrictions than GPT-3.
- Available at: https://huggingface.co/docs/transformers/en/model_doc/gpt2

mT5 (Multilingual T5):

- Focus: Multilingual NLP tasks.
- Available at: https://huggingface.co/docs/transformers/en/model_doc/mt5

XLM-R (Cross-lingual Representation):

- Focus: Cross-lingual understanding and text classification.
- Available at: https://huggingface.co/docs/transformers/en/model_doc/xlm-roberta

These NLP models provide a wide range of options for businesses, developers, and researchers to build applications tailored to specific needs. Choose based on your use case, budget, and required level of customization.

Appendix B

Build a Convolutional Neural Network (CNN) to Detect Defects Using Image Processing

Using OpenCV and TensorFlow, you can build a Convolutional Neural Network (CNN) to detect defects in products or materials by leveraging image processing and deep learning. Here's a step-by-step guide:

1. Set up the environment.

   Install the required libraries:

   pip install opencv-python tensorflow numpy matplotlib

2. Collect and preprocess data.

You need a dataset of images with defects and without defects. Label these images appropriately (for example, defect and no_defect).

Using OpenCV for Preprocessing

1. Load images: Use OpenCV to read images and resize them to a fixed size.

   import cv2

   import os

   import numpy as np

   def load_and_preprocess_images(directory, label, size=(128, 128)):

   images = []

   labels = []

```
for filename in os.listdir(directory):
    filepath = os.path.join(directory, filename)
    img = cv2.imread(filepath)
    if img is not None:
        img = cv2.resize(img, size)  # Resize images
        images.append(img)
        labels.append(label)         # Label: 1 for defect, 0 for no defect
    return np.array(images), np.array(labels)

defect_images, defect_labels = load_and_preprocess_images("data/
defects", 1)

no_defect_images, no_defect_labels = load_and_preprocess_
images("data/no_defects", 0)
```

2. Combine and normalize data.

```
X = np.vstack((defect_images, no_defect_images))
y = np.hstack((defect_labels, no_defect_labels))

# Normalize pixel values to [0, 1]
X = X / 255.0
```

3. Create a CNN Using TensorFlow.

A CNN model will process the image data and classify whether a defect is present.

Build the CNN:

```
import tensorflow as tf
from tensorflow.keras import layers, models
# Define the CNN architecture
model = models.Sequential([
    layers.Conv2D(32, (3, 3), activation='relu', input_shape=(128,
    128, 3)),
```

```
layers.MaxPooling2D((2, 2)),
layers.Conv2D(64, (3, 3), activation='relu'),
layers.MaxPooling2D((2, 2)),
layers.Conv2D(128, (3, 3), activation='relu'),
layers.MaxPooling2D((2, 2)),
layers.Flatten(),
layers.Dense(128, activation='relu'),
layers.Dense(1, activation='sigmoid')  # Binary classification
(defect/no defect)
])

model.compile(optimizer='adam', loss='binary_crossentropy',
metrics=['accuracy'])
```

View the model summary:

```
model.summary()
```

4. Split data and train the model.

   Split the data into training and validation sets.

```
from sklearn.model_selection import train_test_split

X_train, X_val, y_train, y_val = train_test_split(X, y, test_
size=0.2, random_state=42)

# Train the model
history = model.fit(X_train, y_train, epochs=10, validation_
data=(X_val, y_val), batch_size=32)
```

5. Evaluate the model.

   Evaluate the performance of your CNN on the validation data.

```
# Evaluate accuracy and loss
loss, accuracy = model.evaluate(X_val, y_val)
print(f"Validation Accuracy: {accuracy * 100:.2f}%")
```

6. Test the model.

   Use the trained model to predict defects in new images.

   ```
   def predict_defect(image_path):
       img = cv2.imread(image_path)
       img = cv2.resize(img, (128, 128)) / 255.0
       img = np.expand_dims(img, axis=0)  # Add batch dimension
       prediction = model.predict(img)
           return "Defect" if prediction[0][0] > 0.5 else "No Defect"

       # Example usage
       print(predict_defect("test_image.jpg"))
   ```

7. Save and deploy the model.

   Save the trained model for deployment.

   ```
   model.save("defect_detection_model.h5")
   ```

   To deploy:

   a. Integrate the model into a web application using Flask or FastAPI.

   b. Use OpenCV in real-time to capture images from a camera and feed them to the CNN for defect detection.

8. Enhance the pipeline.

   a. Data augmentation: Use TensorFlow or OpenCV to augment your dataset (rotate, flip, scale images).

   ```
   data_augmentation = tf.keras.Sequential([
       layers.RandomFlip("horizontal_and_vertical"),
       layers.RandomRotation(0.2),
   ])
   ```

b. Hyperparameter tuning: Experiment with different learning rates, optimizer types, and CNN architectures.

c. Model optimization for edge devices: Use TensorFlow Lite to optimize the model for mobile or edge deployment.

9. Monitor and make continuous improvements.

- Regularly update the model with new data.
- Use performance metrics like precision, recall, and F1-score to track its effectiveness.

By combining OpenCV for image preprocessing and TensorFlow for deep learning, you can create a robust defect detection system that is scalable and efficient.

Next Steps

CNN architecture: The provided CNN architecture is a basic example. You might want to explore more complex architectures depending on your dataset size and complexity.

Data augmentation example: The data augmentation example shows basic flips and rotations. You can consider adding other techniques like scaling, noise injection, and color jittering for a more robust model.

Deployment details: While the guide mentions deployment options, it could be more specific about frameworks like Flask or FastAPI.

Overall, this is a great guide for getting started with defect detection using OpenCV and TensorFlow. Remember, building a good model might require experimentation and adjustments depending on your specific needs and dataset characteristics.

Appendix C

OpenCV Example of AI Vision Detecting Surface Defects on a Conveyor Belt

1. Capture: The inspection camera captures images of items moving on the production line.

2. Preprocess: Convert the image to grayscale and apply Gaussian blur to reduce noise.

   import cv2

   image = cv2.imread("product_image.jpg")

   gray = cv2.cvtColor(image, cv2.COLOR_BGR2GRAY)

   blurred = cv2.GaussianBlur(gray, (5, 5), 0)

3. Edge detection: Use Canny edge detection to identify defects.

   edges = cv2.Canny(blurred, 50, 150)

   cv2.imshow("Edges", edges)

4. Contour analysis: Identify and highlight defect regions.

   contours, _ = cv2.findContours(edges, cv2.RETR_EXTERNAL, cv2.CHAIN_APPROX_SIMPLE)

   for contour in contours:

   cv2.drawContours(image, [contour], -1, (0, 255, 0), 2)

   cv2.imshow("Defects", image)

   cv2.waitKey(0)

   cv2.destroyAllWindows()

5. Automate action: Trigger alerts or actions (for example, reject the defective product).

Glossary

Anomaly Detection: The process of identifying patterns in data that deviate from the expected norm.

Artificial Intelligence (AI): The simulation of human intelligence in machines that can perform tasks like problem-solving, learning, and decision-making.

Automated Root Cause Analysis (ARCA): Using AI algorithms to quickly identify the underlying causes of quality issues.

Bayesian Networks: A probabilistic graphical model that represents a set of variables and their conditional dependencies using a directed acyclic 1 graph.

Big Data Analytics: The process of analyzing large, complex datasets to extract insights and trends.

Blockchain for Quality Management: A distributed ledger technology that ensures secure, immutable records.

CAPA (Corrective and Preventive Actions): Processes used in quality management to investigate, solve, and prevent quality issues.

Chatbot: An AI-powered conversational interface that interacts with users via text or voice.

ChatGPT: A language model developed by OpenAI capable of generating human-like text for a variety of applications.

Cloud Computing: Delivering computing services over the internet, including storage, databases, and AI tools.

Clustering: A machine learning technique that groups data points into clusters based on their similarity.

Computer Vision: A field of AI that enables machines to interpret and make decisions based on visual data like images or videos.

Convolutional Neural Networks (CNNs): A type of deep learning model designed to analyze visual data.

Data Augmentation: A technique to artificially expand training datasets by applying transformations such as rotation, scaling, or noise addition.

Data Lake: A centralized repository that stores vast amounts of raw data in its native format.

Data Pipeline: A set of automated processes that move and prepare data for analysis or model training.

Decision Tree: A predictive model that maps decisions and their possible outcomes using a tree-like structure.

Deep Learning: A subset of ML that uses neural networks with multiple layers to analyze complex patterns in data.

Digital Twin: A virtual replica of a physical object, process, or system, used for simulation and optimization.

Federated Learning: A technique where AI models are trained across decentralized devices or servers without sharing raw data.

FMEA (Failure Modes and Effects Analysis): A step-by-step approach to identifying and evaluating potential failure modes and their impact on processes or products.

Generative Design: A design process powered by AI where algorithms generate optimized designs based on specified constraints and goals.

Hugging Face: An open-source library providing pre-trained models for natural language processing tasks.

Hyperparameter Tuning: The process of optimizing the parameters that govern the learning process of an AI model.

Image Segmentation: Dividing an image into multiple segments for easier analysis.

IoT (Internet of Things): A network of physical devices connected via the internet to collect and exchange data.

Knowledge Graphs: A data structure that represents entities and their relationships, enabling contextual understanding.

Machine Learning (ML): A subset of AI focused on training models to make predictions or decisions based on data.

Neural Networks: Computing systems inspired by the human brain that are used in AI to recognize patterns and make decisions.

NLP (Natural Language Processing): A field of AI that enables machines to understand, interpret, and generate human language.

OpenCV: An open-source computer vision library that provides tools for image and video analysis.

Predictive Analytics: The use of AI models to predict future outcomes based on historical data.

Predictive Maintenance: Using AI to forecast equipment failure or degradation based on sensor data.

Process Optimization: The use of AI to continuously improve workflows or manufacturing processes.

QMS (Quality Management System): A system that documents and manages quality policies, processes, and responsibilities.

Quality 4.0: The integration of digital technologies like AI, IoT, and big data analytics into quality management.

Real-Time Analytics: The process of analyzing data as they are generated to provide immediate insights.

Reinforcement Learning: A type of AI where agents learn by interacting with their environment and receiving rewards for optimal actions.

Root Cause Analysis: A method used to identify the fundamental cause of a quality issue.

Scikit-learn: An open-source library for machine learning in Python, offering tools for classification, regression, and clustering.

Semantic Analysis: A technique in NLP that analyzes the meaning and relationships of words in context.

Sensor Fusion: Combining data from multiple sensors to provide a comprehensive view of a system.

Sentiment Analysis: The use of NLP to determine the emotional tone behind a body of text.

TensorFlow: An open-source platform for building and training ML models.

Text Mining: The process of extracting valuable information from unstructured text data.

Transfer Learning: A technique in machine learning where knowledge from a pre-trained model is applied to a new, related task.

Virtual Assistant: AI-powered systems that assist with routine tasks, such as answering queries or scheduling.

Virtual Quality Assistants: AI-driven assistants designed to support quality management tasks.

YOLO (You Only Look Once): A real-time object detection framework designed for speed and accuracy.

Endnotes

Chapter 1

1. Cognex VisionPro detects defects using AI-driven computer vision.

2. IBM Maximo Predict monitors equipment health and predicts failures.

3. InfinityQS ProFicient integrates AI to analyze production data and trends.

4. MonkeyLearn applies NLP for sentiment analysis and trend identification.

5. Blue Yonder uses AI/ML for inventory management and risk forecasting.

6. PathAI improves diagnostic imaging, and Atomwise accelerates drug discovery.

7. Tableau + Einstein Discovery offers AI-powered data insights and hidden pattern detection.

8. IntelliRisk and IntelliFMEA from DataReality automates hazard analysis and FMEA with AI tools.

Chapter 2

1. Turing, A. M. (1950). Computing machinery and intelligence. *Mind*, 59(236), 433-460. https://doi.org/10.1093/mind/LIX.236.433.

2. OpenAI. (n.d.). *ChatGPT: Language processing AI*. Retrieved from https://openai.com. IBM. (n.d.). *Watson: AI for data analysis and language processing*. Retrieved from https://www.ibm.com/watson. Amazon. (n.d.). Alexa: Voice assistant AI. Retrieved from https://www.amazon.com/alexa.

3. DeepMind. (n.d.). *AlphaGo: Self-learning AI for the game of Go*. Retrieved from https://deepmind.com/research/highlighted-research/alphago.

4. HAL 9000. (1968). *2001: A Space Odyssey* [Film]. Directed by Stanley Kubrick. Metro-Goldwyn-Mayer.

5. OpenAI. (n.d.). *GPT models*. Retrieved from https://openai.com/.

6. H2O.ai. (n.d.). *H2O clustering tool*. Retrieved from https://www.h2o.ai/ and Scikit-learn. (n.d.). *Anomaly detection module*. Retrieved from https://scikit-learn.org.

7. OpenAI. (n.d.). *Gym: A toolkit for developing reinforcement learning*. Retrieved from https://www.gymlibrary.dev/.

8. OpenAI. (2023). *ChatGPT* [Large language model]. Retrieved from https://openai.com/chatgpt.

Chapter 6

1. OpenAI. (2023). *ChatGPT* [Large language model]. Retrieved from https://openai.com/chatgpt.

2. Microsoft. (n.d.). *Copilot: AI-powered productivity tool*. Retrieved from https://www.microsoft.com/en-us/microsoft-365/copilot.

3. Data Reality. (n.d.). *DataReality.ai: Advanced AI solutions*. Retrieved from https://datareality.ai.

4. IBM SPSS Modeler uses historical data and ML models to predict quality issues before they occur. IBM. (n.d.). *SPSS Modeler: Predictive analytics platform*. Retrieved from https://www.ibm.com/analytics/spss-statistics-software.

5. Cognex VisionPro provides AI-powered computer vision systems for defect detection and compliance monitoring. Cognex. (n.d.). *VisionPro: Machine vision software*. Retrieved from https://www.cognex.com/products/machine-vision/visionpro.

6. AuditBoard automates parts of internal and external audits, identifying non-conformance root causes.

AuditBoard. (n.d.). *Connected risk platform*. Retrieved from https://www.auditboard.com.

7. Microsoft Project Bonsai applies reinforcement learning to optimize manufacturing processes dynamically. Microsoft. (n.d.). *Project Bonsai: AI platform for process optimization*. Retrieved from https://www.microsoft.com/en-us/ai/project-bonsai.

8. Siemens MindSphere uses IoT data to monitor equipment conditions and predict failures. Siemens. (n.d.). *MindSphere: Industrial IoT as a service*. Retrieved from https://new.siemens.com/global/en/products/software/mindsphere.html.

9. GE Digital's Predix Platform creates digital twins for simulating production processes and monitoring systems remotely. E Digital. (n.d.). *Predix platform for digital twins*. Retrieved from https://www.ge.com/digital/applications/digital-twin.

10. Resilinc assesses supplier performance, monitors quality metrics, and predicts risks. Resilinc. (n.d.). *Supplier risk management platform*. Retrieved from https://www.resilinc.com.

11. Autodesk Fusion 360 uses generative design to optimize product workflows and reduce waste. Autodesk. (n.d.). *Fusion 360: Generative design software*. Retrieved from https://www.autodesk.com/products/fusion-360/overview.

12. Tableau with Einstein Discovery integrates AI for scenario simulations and actionable recommendations. Tableau. (n.d.). *Einstein Discovery for decision support*. Retrieved from https://www.tableau.com/products/einstein-discovery.

13. Matrox. (n.d.). *Matrox Imaging Library (MIL): Vision software for automated inspections*. Retrieved from https://www.matrox.com/en/imaging/products/software/mil.

14. Qualtrics. (n.d.). *Customer feedback and sentiment analysis platform*. Retrieved from https://www.qualtrics.com.

15. Amazon Web Services. (n.d.). *AWS IoT Analytics: Predictive maintenance and operational efficiency*. Retrieved from https://aws.amazon.com/iot-analytics/.

Chapter 7

1. Zebra Technologies. (n.d.). *Aurora Vision: AI-powered machine vision software*. Retrieved from https://www.zebra.com/us/en/solutions/vision.html.

2. OpenAI. (2023). *ChatGPT: Language model for automated customer support*. Retrieved from https://openai.com/chatgpt.

Chapter 9

1. Amazon Web Services. (n.d.). *Amazon Comprehend: Natural language processing service*. Retrieved from https://aws.amazon.com/comprehend/.

2. Microsoft. (n.d.). *Azure Machine Learning: AI and machine learning platform*. Retrieved from https://azure.microsoft.com/en-us/services/machine-learning/.

3. Google. (n.d.). *Google Cloud Dataflow: Stream and batch data processing*. Retrieved from https://cloud.google.com/dataflow.

4. Tableau. (n.d.). *Data visualization and analytics platform*. Retrieved from https://www.tableau.com.

5. Amazon Web Services. (n.d.). *Amazon SageMaker: Machine learning service*. Retrieved from https://aws.amazon.com/sagemaker/.

Chapter 10

1. Siemens. (n.d.). *MindSphere: Industrial IoT as a service*. Retrieved from https://new.siemens.com/global/en/products/software/mindsphere.html.

2. IBM. (n.d.). *Maximo Predict: Predictive maintenance solution*. Retrieved from https://www.ibm.com/products/maximo.

3. Rockwell Automation. (n.d.). *FactoryTalk Analytics: Data-driven decision-making for manufacturing*. Retrieved from https://www.rockwellautomation.com/en-us/products/software/factorytalk.html.

4. Honeywell. (n.d.). *Honeywell Forge: Enterprise performance management platform.* Retrieved from https://www. honeywellforge.ai/.

5. Siemens. (n.d.). *MindSphere: Industrial IoT as a service.* Retrieved from https://new.siemens.com/global/en/products/software/ mindsphere.html.

Chapter 12

1. **Implementation of Computer Vision:** The company deployed Cognex VisionPro to install high-resolution cameras along the inspection lines. Machine learning models were trained to detect cracks, uneven surfaces, and material inconsistencies in brake pads. **Integration with Testing Systems:** Using Siemens Simatic IT, the inspection data were integrated with performance testing systems to correlate visual defects with functional failures, enabling better root cause analysis. **Adaptive Testing Strategy:** With Rockwell Automation FactoryTalk Analytics, testing parameters were dynamically adjusted based on defect patterns identified by the machine learning system, ensuring efficient quality control and reducing unnecessary testing.

Chapter 13

1. Amazon Web Services. (n.d.). *AWS IoT Analytics: Real-time IoT data analysis.* Retrieved from https://aws.amazon.com/ iot-analytics/.

2. Simio LLC. (n.d.). *Simio: Simulation and scheduling software.* Retrieved from https://www.simio.com.

3. Microsoft. (n.d.). *Azure Machine Learning: AI pattern recognition.* Retrieved from https://azure.microsoft.com/en-us/services/ machine-learning/.

4. GE Digital. (n.d.). *Predix platform for industrial AI and analytics.* Retrieved from https://www.ge.com/digital/.

5. Using Microsoft Azure AI, a manufacturing plant monitors real-time production data and detects anomalies in cycle times. Microsoft. (n.d.). *Azure AI: AI and machine learning solutions.* Retrieved from https://azure.microsoft.com/en-us/.

6. A logistics company utilizes UiPath Process Mining to analyze workflows and identify common Lean wastes. UiPath. (n.d.). *Process mining for workflow optimization.* Retrieved from https://www.uipath.com/product/process-mining.

7. Tableau with Einstein Discovery generates automated heat maps and visualizations that highlight bottlenecks and delays in production. Tableau. (n.d.). *Data visualization and AI-driven insights.* Retrieved from https://www.tableau.com.

8. Microsoft. (n.d.). *Power Automate: Workflow automation and process optimization.* Retrieved from https://powerautomate.microsoft.com/.

9. Minit. (n.d.). *Process mining and analysis platform.* Retrieved from https://minit.io/.

10. IBM. (n.d.). *Process Mining: Discover, visualize, and optimize workflows.* Retrieved from https://www.ibm.com/products/process-mining.

11. Lucid Software. (n.d.). *Lucidchart: Visual workspace for diagramming and process mapping.* Retrieved from https://www.lucidchart.com/.

12. UiPath. (n.d.). *Process Mining for workflow optimization.* Retrieved from https://www.uipath.com/product/process-mining/.

Chapter 14

1. SAP. (n.d.). *SAP Ariba: Supplier performance and risk management.* Retrieved from https://www.sap.com/products/ariba.html.

2. Honeywell. (n.d.). *Honeywell Forge: IoT-enabled quality monitoring platform.* Retrieved from https://www.honeywellforge.ai.

3. IBM. (n.d.). Maximo Predict: Predictive maintenance and quality management. Retrieved from https://www.ibm.com/products/maximo.

4. Coupa. (n.d.). *Coupa supplier management platform*. Retrieved from https://www.coupa.com.

5. IBM. (n.d.). *IBM Food Trust: Blockchain for supply chain transparency*. Retrieved from https://www.ibm.com/products/food-trust.

6. DHL. (n.d.). *SmartSensor: IoT-enabled temperature tracking for logistics*. Retrieved from https://www.dhl.com/global-en/home/our-divisions/solutions/dhl-smart-sensor.html.

7. SAP. (n.d.). *SAP Integrated Business Planning (IBP): Planning and risk simulation tool*. Retrieved from https://www.sap.com/products/integrated-business-planning.html.

8. Siemens. (n.d.). *MindSphere: Industrial IoT as a service*. Retrieved from https://new.siemens.com/global/en/products/software/mindsphere.html.

9. SAP. (n.d.). *SAP Ariba: Supplier performance and risk management*. Retrieved from https://www.sap.com/products/ariba.html.

10. IBM. (n.d.). *Planning Analytics with Watson*. Retrieved from https://www.ibm.com/products/planning-analytics.

11. Oracle. (n.d.). *Blockchain platform for supply chain traceability*. Retrieved from https://www.oracle.com/blockchain/.

12. Amazon Web Services. (n.d.). *AWS IoT Core: IoT management platform*. Retrieved from https://aws.amazon.com/iot-core/.

Chapter 15

1. International Organization for Standardization. (2022). *ISO/IEC 22989:2022 - Information technology—Artificial intelligence—Artificial intelligence concepts and terminology*. International Organization for Standardization.

2. International Organization for Standardization. (2023). *ISO/IEC 23894:2023 - Information technology—Artificial intelligence—Guidance on risk management*. International Organization for Standardization.

3. IBM. (n.d.). *OpenPages with Watson: AI-driven risk management platform*. Retrieved from https://www.ibm.com/products/openpages/.

4. Data Reality. (n.d.). *DataReality.ai: AI-powered data solutions*. Retrieved from https://datareality.ai.

5. CrowdStrike. (n.d.). *Falcon: AI-driven threat detection and prevention platform*. Retrieved from https://www.crowdstrike.com.

6. Tenable. (n.d.). *Tenable.io: Predictive vulnerability management solution*. Retrieved from https://www.tenable.com/products/tenable-io.

7. Palo Alto Networks. (n.d.). *Cortex XSOAR: Security orchestration and automated response platform*. Retrieved from https://www.paloaltonetworks.com/cortex/xsoar.

8. Darktrace. (n.d.). *Enterprise Immune System: AI-powered cybersecurity monitoring solution*. Retrieved from https://www.darktrace.com.

9. Data Reality. (n.d.). *DataReality.ai: AI-powered data solutions*. Retrieved from https://datareality.ai.

Chapter 16

1. STRIVR. (n.d.). *STRIVR: Immersive learning and skill assessment platform*. Retrieved from https://www.strivr.com.

2. Cornerstone OnDemand. (n.d.). *Certification and compliance management solutions*. Retrieved from https://www.cornerstoneondemand.com.

3. Kahoot!. (n.d.). *Kahoot! for Business: Gamified learning and engagement platform*. Retrieved from https://kahoot.com/business.

4. M-Files. (n.d.). *Intelligent document management system*. Retrieved from https://www.m-files.com.

5. Bloomfire. (n.d.). *Knowledge management and collaboration software*. Retrieved from https://bloomfire.com.

6. Syntheia. (n.d.). *Knowledge capture and management solution.* Retrieved from https://syntheia.com.

7. Atlassian. (n.d.). *Confluence: Team collaboration and knowledge management platform.* Retrieved from https://www.atlassian.com/software/confluence.

Chapter 18

1. GE Digital. (n.d.). *Predix: Industrial IoT platform.* Retrieved from https://www.ge.com/digital.

2. TIBCO. (n.d.). *Spotfire: Data visualization and analytics platform.* Retrieved from https://www.tibco.com/products/spotfire.

3. ANSYS. (n.d.). *ANSYS simulation software.* Retrieved from https://www.ansys.com.

4. SAP. (n.d.). *Predictive maintenance and service solutions.* Retrieved from https://www.sap.com/products/predictive-maintenance-service.html.

5. ANSYS. (n.d.). *Fluent: AI-powered fluid simulation software.* Retrieved from https://www.ansys.com/products/fluids/ansys-fluent.

6. Minitab. (n.d.). *Engage: Design of experiments and optimization tool.* Retrieved from https://www.minitab.com/en-us/products/engage.

7. Autodesk. (n.d.). *Fusion 360: AI-enhanced CAD simulation software.* Retrieved from https://www.autodesk.com/products/fusion-360/overview.

8. Siemens. (n.d.). *Simcenter: Digital twin and simulation platform.* Retrieved from https://www.plm.automation.siemens.com/global/en/products/simcenter/.

9. Amazon Web Services. (n.d.). *AWS IoT Analytics: IoT data processing and analytics platform.* Retrieved from https://aws.amazon.com/iot-analytics/.

10. IBM. (n.d.). *Watson IoT Platform: Predictive maintenance and reliability tool.* Retrieved from https://www.ibm.com/internet-of-things.

11. Siemens. (n.d.). *MindSphere: IoT and AI platform for reliability management.* Retrieved from https://new.siemens.com/global/en/products/software/mindsphere.html.